*Folger Documents of Tudor
and Stuart Civilization*

A DISCOURSE OF THE COMMONWEAL

OF THIS REALM OF ENGLAND

Folger Documents
of Tudor and Stuart Civilization

THIS volume is one of a series of publications of Tudor and Stuart documents that the Folger Library proposes to bring out. These documents will consist of hitherto unprinted manuscripts as well as reprints of rare books in the Folger Library. An effort will be made to choose significant items that will throw light on the social and intellectual background of the period from 1485 to 1715. In response to almost unanimous requests of interested historians, the spelling, punctuation, and capitalization will be modernized in printed texts. In some cases, where the original printing is clear and easily read, texts may be photographically reproduced.

The Folger Shakespeare Library is administered by the Trustees of Amherst College.

A Discourse of the Commonweal of This Realm of England

Attributed to Sir Thomas Smith

EDITED BY MARY DEWAR

Published for
The Folger Shakespeare Library

The University Press of Virginia
Charlottesville

Preface

A Discourse of the Commonweal of This Realm of England was first printed in 1581 in London by T. Marshe. It was reprinted several times: in 1751 by Charles Marsh; in 1808 in the *Harleian Miscellany*, Vol. IX; in 1813 in the *Pamphleteer*, Vol. V; and in 1876 in the New Shakspere Society, Series VI, No. 3. In 1893 E. Lamond published an earlier manuscript copy of the work, the Lambarde manuscript now in the possession of University College, London. This edition of 1893, reprinted in 1929 and 1954, differed in many respects from the printed text of 1581, for alterations had been made in the latter, sections added and deleted. This edition for the Folger Series is from another manuscript text, the Yelverton manuscript, now B.M. Add. MS 48047 ff. 174–227. Of the five early manuscript copies of the *Discourse* known, this text has the fewest omissions and errors and is closest to the original text. A discussion of the manuscript texts and their relation to the first printed edition will be found in Appendix B. The manuscript texts and the printed edition are identified throughout as follows:

The printed edition of 1581	(S)
The Lambarde MS	(L)
The Yelverton MS (B.M. Add. MS 48047 ff. 174–227)	(Y)
The Bodleian MS (Add. C. 273)	(B)
The Hatfield MS (269/2)	(H)
The Albany MS	(A)

As in all the books in this series the spelling and punctuation have been modernized, although certain archaic words which are an inalienable part of Tudor English have been retained. Verb endings have been modernized, e.g., "hath" to "has," "seemeth" to "seems." Latin words and phrases have been left in their original spelling and where necessary translated in footnotes. So far as possible the characteristic complex sentence structure of the original has been maintained. Three types of alterations to the Yelverton manuscript have been made. Firstly, where the clerk has clearly made a careless copying error such as an omission of a word (or on three or four occasions omission of an entire phrase) and the other manuscript texts supply the missing or obviously correct words, these have been inserted in the text enclosed in square brackets. Secondly, the marginal notes have been moved to the bottom of the page with symbols denoting the relevant passage in the text. Thirdly, in addition to putting the names of the speakers in the margin the Yelverton manuscript inserts into the opening sentence of every speech a "quoth I" or "quoth the Doctor," etc. The effect is tedious and mildly irritating; nothing seemed lost by removing these unnecessary interjections except when clarity or style dictated that they should be retained.

Notes to the text have been mainly confined to the explanation of archaic words, Latin translations, and brief identifications of people and incidents mentioned by the author.

The authorship of the *Discourse*, its date, and the alterations made to the text for the first printing of 1581 are discussed in the Introduction.

MARY DEWAR

The University of Texas
December 12, 1968

Contents

Introduction

In times of accelerated economic change and widespread social dislocation nothing flourishes more than the literature of complaint, of analysis, of exhortation, and of blame. *A Discourse of the Commonweal of This Realm of England,* written in 1549 and first published in 1581, was the most brilliant and most enduring of an overwhelming flood of pamphlets, books, sermons, poems, and treatises prompted by the severe inflation and changing economic patterns of Tudor England.[1]

The rise in prices in sixteenth-century England was relentless and at times severe. From 1500 to 1540 prices rose by a half and doubled in the next twenty years. By the 1580's prices were three and a half times the 1500 level. In 1600 they were five and a half times higher than at the beginning of the century. This upward movement of prices was a complex phenomenon. It was not a steady rise; at times, especially in the twenty years from 1540 to 1560, it was unexpectedly swift and savage, shaking the whole economic framework and proving a shattering experience to all who experienced it. Prices which had risen some 40

[1] Examples of this literary "explosion" can be found in R. H. Tawney and E. Power, *Tudor Economic Documents* (London, New York, 1924, 1953), III.

per cent in the thirties rose by 77 per cent in the forties and by 155 per cent in the fifties. It hurt most people; it was a catastrophe for the poor. The general dislocation of the economy brought hardship to farmers, landowners, merchants, and other classes. It gave all a deep sense of grievance. It is to this period of sharp inflation, 1540 to 1560, that most of the protest literature belongs, the *Discourse* being written at the height of the storm in 1549.

The causes of this price rise throughout the century (and indeed throughout Western Europe) are still the subject of argument and controversy, as they were the occasion of bitter debate at the time. It is now clear that many factors contributed to drive prices upwards. The primary cause was a steadily mounting population which, along with increased urbanization, put growing pressure on all natural resources, especially food supplies. Population statistics for the sixteenth century are nonexistent, scanty, or totally unreliable, but it can be estimated that the population rose in England from a low of about two million at the end of the fourteenth century to something over three million by the 1540's, a rise echoed in Western Europe. Such an increase in population inevitably raised food prices until more productive methods of farming and more ruthless exploitation of the land could satisfy the new demands. There were other factors at work which helped inflation along, exaggerated its effects, and were, in turn, affected by it. There was an increased amount of money available, and its circulation was faster than before. The discovery of new silver mines in Europe and later more efficient methods of extracting the ore increased Europe's stocks of its main monetary metal. Later still both gold and silver were to pour in an increasing stream from the newly discovered mines of the Americas, a stream which Spain spread over all Europe through trade, war, and the imperial activities of her rulers. New monetary and business techniques, including new credit facilities, also increased the velocity of circulation of money which acted to put pressure on prices. In England monetary stocks were also increased by a favorable trade balance from 1500 to 1540, an export surplus paid for in cash. The mint also profited from the plate and bullion seized by the crown from the confiscated property of the church. To these increased stocks of money, readily available, were added other inflationary pressures. Increasingly heavy crown expenditure for all purposes including war acted to drive prices upwards. All these factors—heavy population, increased urbanization, growing stocks of money, increased velocity of circulation, heavy government spending—operated to a greater or less degree throughout the century. The problem became acute and brought the country to a state of crisis in the forties and fifties because the crown piled on top of all these factors a series of drastic and totally disastrous debasements of the coinage.[2] From 1540 to 1551 the silver content of the coinage was reduced by two thirds and the gold content by a quarter. The results were catastrophic. Faced with these lighter coins, of baser metal, the people refused to take them at their face value, confidence in the value of money was shaken, and the inevitable happened; prices rocketed.

If the primary causes of the price rise have been a subject for speculation and argument for so long it is not surprising that those living through it found it even harder to explain. What was certain was that inflation brought hardship to many and a grievance to all; "every man," said the author of the *Discourse*, "finds himself grieved." [3]

Social and economic patterns shifted under its pressure and in turn accelerated its effect. Landlords were anxious to use new techniques which would improve the commercial exploitation of their lands. In a few areas this called for heavy enclosure of land and a change-over from crop growing to sheep farming in response to the growing demand for wool and mutton at home and, for a prolonged period, an expanding market for wool and unfinished cloth abroad. Some agricultural laborers were accordingly squeezed out

---

[2] Notably in 1542, 1544, 1546, 1549, and 1551.
[3] See *Discourse*, p. 33.

of their small holdings, and where this occurred the disturbance of established agrarian communities caused a good deal of hardship.[4] As well as adopting new methods of land use, landlords increased the entry "fines," chargeable whenever leases fell in, and raised rents wherever possible. All who could sell land at the new inflated values did so, causing more disturbance of established communities. The crown, as the biggest rentier of all, was the worst hit. In the early 1540's it feverishly sold the recently acquired monastic lands, and then was driven to heavy debasement of the coinage in a series of vain and disastrous attempts to meet its chronic shortage of money.

The fall in the real value of money brought instability to the increasingly important industrial and mercantile community as well as to the nine-tenths of the population which still lived on the land. England's commercial life revolved round the export of wool and unfinished cloth which had experienced boom conditions in the early decades of the century. In the late 1550's the demand from abroad fell off and soon merchants and unemployed clothworkers added their cries of complaint to those of the displaced agricultural laborer and harassed landlord.

"The towns go down, the land decays" [5] —one could imagine that utter desolation overtook the whole realm. In sober fact it was not so. Steadily national wealth was increasing under improved methods of land management, new industries, and new commercial and monetary techniques. But the suffering was real. To those sections of society hit by change the catastrophe was complete; to all fighting a losing battle against inflation the times seemed harsh. To

---

[4] Although the extent of such enclosure is now known to have been relatively small, it could have dramatic effects locally and one village so affected could easily become that widespread "desolation" of the countryside of which the husbandman speaks so bitterly: "where forty persons had their livings, now one man and his shepherd has all." See *Discourse*, p. 17.

[5] From the ballad "Now a Days," *ca.* 1520, quoted in Tawney and Power, *op. cit.*, III, 19. (Spelling has been modernized.)

everyone this "marvelous dearth[6] that in such plenty comes"[7] was a source of bewilderment.

Cause and effect were easily confused. The laborers displaced by sheep farming saw no flaw in the simple formula: "The more sheep, the fewer eggs for a penny." [8] A landlord raising rents to meet the higher prices was soon regarded as a prime mover in raising costs:

> For if the farmer pay fourfold double rent,
> He must his ware needs sell after that stint.[9]

All sought villains for the piece, the pamphleteer as readily as the "landless commons" turning out to tear down the enclosing fences. The poor, the dispossessed, the harassed had no doubt that those who seemed to prosper could only have done so at the expense of society as a whole. Sermons thundered against the greed and covetousness of men. A natural dislike of unpleasant change was reinforced by traditional modes of thought and men turned to the old ideal of the "true commonweal" in which the common good overrode private interest, where no man would pursue his own profit to the harm of others but would readily do "that which he sees shall be for the quietness of the realm, albeit his private profit bids him do the contrary." [10] It was this concept of an ideal commonwealth against which present reality could be judged which gave the protest literature of the time, however varied, a recognizable personality and a

---

[6] Throughout the *Discourse* "dearth" is used in its old sense of "dearness," not its modern meaning of scarcity; see the Knight's comment (p. 37) "dearth of all things though there be scarcity of nothing."

[7] See *Discourse*, p. 38.

[8] From "The Decay of England only by the Great Multitude of Sheep," 1550–53, quoted in Tawney and Power, *op. cit.*, III, 52. (Spelling has been modernized.)

[9] From William Forrest's, "The Pleasant Poesy of Princely Practice," 1548, *ibid.*, p. 40.

[10] R. Morison, *A Remedy for Sedition* (1536), sig. A4r. (STC 20877). A recent ed. is that by E. M. Cox (London, 1933).

name. Of this "commonwealth literature," much of it mere protest, much of it backward looking, or of no lasting merit, the *Discourse of the Commonweal* with its unexampled analysis of the troubled times has deservedly been called "the movement's literary monument." [11]

The *Discourse* sets out to analyze the causes of "the manifold complaints of men touching the decay of this Commonweal"; first to find out "what things men are most grieved with," secondly "what should be the occasion of the same," and thirdly "that known, how such griefs may be taken away and the state of the Commonweal reformed again." The author uses the dramatic literary device of an imaginary conversation between five persons pursuing their own grievances with vigor. As the "Knight," the "Merchant," the "Capper," and the "Husbandman" move into attack, argue their case, and propose their remedies, the learned "Doctor" probes their arguments, shows the weaknesses in their accusations, reveals the common factors underlying their experiences, and finally elicits their common agreement to his own analysis of the situation. No problem escapes the five characters and nowhere else can one find such a revealing picture of the problems and grievances of the time. It is not surprising that for four hundred years the book has been regarded as a leading source of information on the social conditions of Tudor England.

Relentlessly the Doctor demonstrates that all classes are victims of the same inflationary process which he traces to the debasement of the coinage: "The alteration of the coin should be the very cause of this dearth and consequently of other griefs." "And thus to conclude, I think this alteration of the coin to be the first original cause; that strangers first sell their wares dearer to us and that makes all farmers and tenants that rear any commodity again to sell the same dearer, the dearth thereof makes the gentlemen to sell their rents and to take farms to their hands for their better provision and consequently to enclose more ground." No other

---

[11] S. T. Bindoff, *Tudor England* (Harmondsworth, 1950), p. 130.

contemporary writer saw so clearly the far-reaching conse-
quences of the debasements of the coinage which were re-
sponsible for making the 1540's and 1550's the most disastrous and difficult years of the century.[12]

When the book was finally published thirty-two years
later the continued rise in prices, despite the ending of debasement by the Elizabethan recoinage measures of the
1560's, had to be explained. An addition to the original text [13]
ascribed it partly to continued rack-renting but more to the
influx of treasure into the country from the New World,
an analysis which was highly novel at the time [14] and has
only very recently been even partly challenged.[15] It is
hardly surprising that the *Discourse* has been described as

[12] Although it is now acknowledged that deeper factors underlay
the inflationary process throughout the century, recent studies con-
firm that the debasements had a major and "lasting" effect; see Y. S.
Brenner, "The Inflation of Prices in Early Sixteenth Century England," *Economic History Review*, 2nd ser., XIV (1961–62), 225–39,
and the conclusion of J. D. Gould that with a wider understanding
of the complexity of the problem "one can restore to its rightful position the debasement of the English coinage in the years following
1543," from "The Price Revolution Reconsidered," *ibid.*, 2nd ser.,
XVII (1964–65), 265.

[13] See Appendix A, part II. The section which it replaced runs from
p. 102 to p. 116 and is enclosed in **.

[14] It was probably not entirely original. In 1568 Jean Bodin published *La Réponse de Maistre Jean Bodin* in which the suggestion
was first made that the price rise could be so explained, a suggestion
which was amplified in his second edition of 1578. However, the author of the *Discourse* was certainly the first to give circulation to the
idea in English.

[15] See J. D. Gould, *op. cit.*, p. 249: "Until a few years ago historians
of the sixteenth and seventeenth centuries knew that one of the major
phenomena of their period was a secular decline in the value of money
which was so general and so marked as to justify the title 'The Price
Revolution.' They knew further, that this fall in the value of money
was very largely caused by an influx of silver from the Spanish colonial acquisitions in the New World to Europe. . . . Some historians
are still satisfied with this 'orthodox' interpretation of the sixteenth
and seventeenth centuries, but others have recently been assailed by
doubts as to its validity."

"the most advanced statement of economic thought in Tudor England." [16]

Indeed the *Discourse* is a far cry from much of the backward-looking commonwealth literature. It moves firmly toward a new conception of the social process. Most of the "literature of the commonweal" found it difficult to abandon a static conception of society. It accepted economic change with reluctance, and where this appeared to be prompted by sectional self-interest or personal advantage it viewed the changes with suspicious dislike and lurking moral disapprobation. The *Discourse* however recognizes self-interest as a perfectly acceptable force which intelligent government action should direct toward the common good. [17] Men naturally and properly "seek where most advantage is"; if their actions should prove "hurtful to others" (as had to be conceded at times, e.g., enclosure) then the problem was simply "how to bring them that they would not do so." Such deflection was not best done "by the straight penalties of the law" but "by allurement and rewards rather." Men could be "provoked with lucre" to shape their activities toward the common good of society. The hardship caused by enclosure could be prevented by ensuring that "the profit of the plow" be made "as good, rate for rate, as the profit of the grazier and the sheepmaster." How could this be done? —again, not by elaborate rules, regulations, and penalties but by removing the existing restrictions on the sale of corn and giving corn growers "liberty to sell it at all times and to all places as freely as men may do other things." The *Discourse* thus expresses a more dynamic conception of society; one in which economic forces and individual self-interest would, if freed and encouraged, contribute automatically to national prosperity and common well-being. Succeeding

[16] G. Unwin, quoted by E. Hughes in "The Authorship of the Discourse of the Commonweal," *Bulletin of the John Rylands Library,* XXI (1937), 168.

[17] For a discussion of this aspect of the *Discourse,* see A. B. Ferguson, "The Tudor Commonweal and the Sense of Change," *Journal of British Studies,* III, no. 1 (Nov., 1963), 11–35.

generations of English economic thinkers were to read the *Discourse* with a sense of familiarity and approval of its basic premises which was not aroused by most of the literature of the commonweal.

Contemporary comment on social and economic problems can quickly sound naïve and irrelevant to later generations. However to anyone aware of the discussion of the perils and problems of inflation in twentieth-century, postwar Britain, the *Discourse* reads with startling and mildly disconcerting familiarity. All complain of rising prices in only too well-known terms. The landlords and all who "have their livings and stipends rated at a certainty" are convinced that they are the worst sufferers. They cannot keep up their lavish households as they were used to, which in the past gave such useful employment to so many and enhanced the social scene. The manufacturer complains that he has to pay more than double the old wages, but still his journeymen "say they cannot sufficiently live thereon." It is true, all admit, that crop yields have been excellent, "one acre bearing as much corn as two most commonly were wont to do," but still prices increase. It is suggested that much of the trouble comes from the rising expectations and insatiable desires of the lower classes; "nowadays servingmen go more costly in apparel and look to fare more daintily than their masters were wont to do in times past." The love of foreign luxury goods, the import of which costs "inestimable treasure every year," is deplored. The only solution is to maintain a better balance of trade: "We must always take heed that we buy no more of strangers than we do sell them, for so we should impoverish ourselves and enrich them." Home industries need protection from foreign competition; the case of the papermaker is cited who had to abandon its manufacture because he could not sell it "as good cheap as that came from beyond the seas." Export industries "which bring in treasure" are "most to be cherished." The export of raw materials should be discouraged and new home industries founded. By the time the reader has heard the complaints about rising rents and speculation in property, of the resistance of native workers to any influx of foreign labor, of the cautious hostility of the closed craft organizations, of the exhortations for better quality export goods, etc., the refrain has become altogether too familiar. One is almost prepared for the suggestion that "the exhausting of the treasure of this realm" may even have something to do with a falling off in the national character, "our sloth," "our idleness which we Englishmen percase [18] use more than other nations."

The *Discourse* was first published in 1581 by Thomas Marshe, printer of London, under the title *A Compendious or Brief Examination of Certain Ordinary Complaints of Divers of Our Countrymen in These Our Days, Which Although They Are in Some Part Unjust & Frivolous, Yet Are They All by Way of Dialogues Thoroughly Debated & Discussed. By W. S. Gentleman.* The identity of the author caused immediate speculation and has continued to do so.[19] One knowledgeable contemporary however was not interested in "W. S." William Lambarde, the Kentish antiquary, recorded on his manuscript copy of the *Discourse* that "W. S. " was not the author:

Note, that this book was published in print under the title of A Brief Conceit of English Policy, by one W. S. in the year 1581. Whereas it was long since penned by Sir Thomas Smythe (as some say) or Mr. John Hales (as others think) either in the reign of H.8. or E. the 6. And I myself have long had this copy of it which I caused to be written out, in the year 1565.[20]

[18] *Percase:* perhaps.

[19] Perhaps the most enterprising suggestion was made by Charles Marsh, the editor of the 1751 edition, who announced with a fine disregard of chronology that "this treatise of English policy was composed by the most extensive and fertile genius that ever any age or nation produced, the inimitable Shakespeare." For some time the suggestion made by Anthony à Wood at the end of the seventeenth century that "W. S." was "William Stafford" received some credence until discredited by Dr. Furnivall in 1876 and later also by Miss E. Lamond. For a full account of speculations on the authorship up to 1934, see J. Y. Le Branchu, *Ecrits notables sur la Monnaie, XVI*e *Siècle* (Paris, 1934), I, lxxvii–lxxx.

[20] Lambarde MS in the possession of University College, London.

Lambarde was correct in saying that it was an earlier book. Several precise references in the text pin point the date to the late summer, August and September, of 1549. The *Discourse* opens with a mention of the activities of the great enclosure commission of 1548. In 1548 Somerset, the Lord Protector, had issued a proclamation forbidding further enclosures and had appointed six commissioners to hold inquests in the midland counties where most of the recent enclosing had taken place and was causing unrest. In the following summer of 1549 the commission was very active and in many places the hopes of redress raised by the commission provoked sporadic outbursts and disturbances. The Doctor further refers to a current tax on cloth made within the realm, "12*d*. in every pound in the last subsidy." [21] The summer months of 1549 were the only ones in which this tax could have been described as being in force. The Act of February, 1549, "For the Relief of Subsidy of Goods, Sheep, and Clothes for Three Years," [22] put a tax on home-produced cloth but agitation for the repeal of the Act began as early as November, 1549. The *Discourse* also mentions a recent ban on "stage plays, interludes, May games, wakes, [and] revels," etc., which again ties in with a summer proclamation of 1549 for the "inhibition of Players." [23] Other comments on coinage, the scandal of the carriage of the old gold coinage out of the country (which was inveighed against by a proclamation of April 11, 1549), the growing import of counterfeit money from abroad, the valuation of the angel at thirty groats, etc., all point to the same period.[24]

[21] He has the figure wrong. The act put a tax of 8*d*. in the pound, not 12*d*.

[22] *Statutes of the Realm* (London, 1810–22), IV, pt. 1, 78–93 (2 and 3 Ed. VI, cap. 36).

[23] "Prohibiting Plays and Interludes," Westminster, Aug. 6, 1549 (3 Ed. VI). See Robert Steele, ed., *Tudor and Stuart Proclamations, 1485–1714* (Oxford, 1910), I, 38, no. 365.

[24] For further discussion of the evidence for dating the *Discourse* to the late summer of 1549, see E. Lamond, *A Discourse of the Common Weal of This Realm of England* (Cambridge, 1893; repr. 1929 and 1954), and J. Y. Le Branchu, *op. cit.*, I, lxiii.

The rival claims of John Hales and Sir Thomas Smith to the authorship of the *Discourse,* begun by Lambarde, have continued to be the subject of much argument.[25] For some time John Hales, Clerk of the Hanaper under Edward VI and the chief member of the Enclosure Commission of 1548, held the field. More recent knowledge of Sir Thomas Smith's life [26] and an examination of his other writings reveal however that the arguments for his having written the *Discourse* are far more compelling.[27]

Sir Thomas Smith (1513–77) was one of the most interesting of those academic scholars who found themselves drawn irresistibly into the wider field of government service in Tudor England. Before the age of thirty he had risen rapidly to the Vice-Chancellorship of Cambridge University, having been in turn reader in Greek and Greek philosophy, a distinguished university orator, and holder of the first Regius Chair of Civil Law. "Sir Thomas Smith [was] in my time," said Richard Eden the famous geographer, "the flower of the University of Cambridge." [28]

A somewhat checkered political career followed in the varying fortunes of the reigns of Edward VI, Mary, and Elizabeth. He was Principal Secretary to Edward VI and to Elizabeth; a Member of Parliament under Edward, Mary, and Elizabeth; several times ambassador to France; Privy Councillor; and Chancellor of the Order of the Garter. "Few Englishmen," it has been said, "have held so many of-

---

[25] Notably by E. Lamond, who reproduced the Lambarde text of the *Discourse,* unfortunately a corrupt and very inaccurate manuscript, and argued that John Hales was the author. J. Y. Le Branchu in 1934 reviewed E. Lamond's arguments and concluded that Smith was more likely to have written the work than Hales. E. Hughes in 1937 also argued that the weight of evidence was for Smith.

[26] M. Dewar, *Sir Thomas Smith: A Tudor Intellectual in Office* (London, 1964).

[27] M. Dewar, "The Authorship of the 'Discourse of the Commonweal,'" *Economic History Review,* 2nd ser., XIX (1966), 388–400.

[28] Preface by Richard Eden to Martin Cortes, *The Art of Navigation* (1561), p. 1.

fices of such different sorts." ²⁹ Early in Edward's reign he
attached himself to the all powerful Lord Protector of the
Realm, the Duke of Somerset, rose high in Somerset's service, and appeared destined for powerful office. He never
quite regained his position after the fall of Somerset, and,
although he several times gained Elizabeth's approval, especially after his brilliant French embassy of 1572 which led
to the Treaty of Blois, he never fully gained her confidence
and the offices which she bestowed brought him little real
power and influence.

The varying fortunes of Smith's public career were only
one side of his life. Always he maintained that wide intellectual interest in many and varied subjects which even as a
youth had dazzled his university contemporaries. Like the
Doctor in the *Discourse* he had nothing but scorn for those
"which can talk nothing but the faculty that they profess."
He read six languages and studied astronomy, mathematics,
chemistry, and medicine as well as the more conventional
fields of theology, philosophy, and law. He was passionately
interested in architecture and designed one of the most "advanced" country houses of the day. His written works cover
a surprising variety of topics: the new pronunciation of
Greek,³⁰ an attempt to revolutionize the writing and spelling
of the English language,³¹ a historical treatise on the value of
Roman money,³² a dialogue on the dangers of Elizabeth's un-

²⁹ F. W. Maitland, preface to *De Republica Anglorum*, ed. L. Alston (Cambridge, 1906), p. x.
³⁰ *De recta & emendata linguae Graecae pronuntiatione Thomas
Smith Angli, tunc in academia Cantabrigiensi publici praelectoris ad
vintoniensem episcopum epistola* (1568), "Cantabrigiae, 12. Aug.
1542."
³¹ *De recta & emendata linguae Anglicae scriptione, dialogus.* This
work also was written in 1542 and published in 1568.
³² A treatise on "The Wages of a Roman Footsoldier" (1562).
There are three manuscript copies of this work, which was never
published: an incomplete seventeenth-century copy (B.M. Harleian
MS 660/35); a copy entitled "A Treatise on the Money of the Romans, dedicated to Sir William Cecil, Kt., Chief Secretary to the
Queen's Majesty" (Soc. of Antiquaries, London, MS 116/1); and a
copy in a volume of Smith's works (B.M. Add. MS 48047, ff. 136–68).

married state,[33] a book of poems and translations of the Psalms,[34] a book of propaganda for his schemes for the colonization of Ireland [35] which has been described as "the first direct printed publicity in England for any business venture," [36] and above all, the *De Republica Anglorum or a Discourse on the Commonwealth of England.*[37] This last book surveyed the government of England, its legal system, and society and analyzed the machinery of the state. "No one," said F. W. Maitland, "would think of writing about the England of Elizabeth's day without paying heed to what was written about that matter by her learned and accomplished Secretary of State." [38]

To anyone familiar with these works of Smith, the *Discourse* is unmistakably from his pen. Both in style and content it echoes his other writings. The Doctor is the mouthpiece for the author's views, and all Smith's cherished beliefs, opinions, and personal quirks emerge in the speeches of the Doctor.[39] Like the Doctor he held the strongest views on the folly and perils of debasement, believing it to be the sole cause of high prices and an especial disaster to the crown.[40] Like the Doctor he believed that there was a "natural" proportion of gold to silver in the coinage which inevitably as-

[33] "Dialogue on the Queen's Marriage" (1561) printed in J. Strype, *Life of the Learned Sir Thomas Smith, Kt.* (1698; Oxford ed., 1820), Appendix, III, 184–259.

[34] B.M. Royal MS 17A, XVII, ed. B. Danielsson, *Stockholm Studies in English XII, Sir Thomas Smith: Literary and Linguistic Works . . . Part I* (Stockholm, 1963).

[35] *A Letter Sent by I. B. Gentleman unto his very friend, Master R. C. Esquire, wherein is contained a large discourse of the peopling & inhabiting the country called the Ardes* (1571).

[36] H. M. Jones, "Origins of the Colonial Idea in England," American Philosophical Society, *Proceedings,* LXXXV (1942), 448–65.

[37] Written in 1565; first published in 1583; ed. L. Alston (Cambridge), 1906.

[38] F. W. Maitland, *op. cit.,* p. vii.

[39] M. Dewar, "The Authorship."

[40] See the treatise on "The Wages of a Roman Footsoldier" where Smith develops his theme that "the abating of the standard is a manifest token of the decay of the state and a continual undoing unto it, for as the money abases so do all things enhance."

serted itself throughout the ages. Both emphasized the necessity of a wide humanistic learning, not technical expertise in
one subject; both deplored the hasty judgment of the young
in matters such as religion and law. Both thought disputation
in religion a profitless task for laymen and preferred theo-
logical dispute to remain the quiet preserve of churchmen.
On economic matters both wished to check the export of
raw wool from the realm and encourage the manufacture of
clothing within the country. The author betrays a familiarity with details of the clothing trade as befits one whose
father and brother were "drapers." He reveres the civil law,
acidly deplores extravagance of clothing and the maintenance of luxurious establishments, but shows a mild indul-
gence toward Smith's own failing of ostentatious and ex-
travagant expenditure on domestic architecture.[41]

The very occasion of the book is characteristic of Smith.
In the summer of 1549 he was Principal Secretary and much
concerned with the country's financial and economic affairs.
He had fallen temporarily out of favor with the Lord Protector and had been ordered to leave the Court and to retire
to his residence at Eton College where he was then Provost.
His Secretarial work was taken over by Cecil while he was
left chafing in unwelcome idle seclusion at a time when social disturbances were sweeping the countryside. Somerset
appeared incapable of bringing stability to the country's fi-
nances or order to the realm. He had rejected all criticism or
advice. Specifically he had swept aside Smith's own sugges-
tions as to how the various problems should be handled.[42]

Throughout his life Smith's reaction to this sort of situation was as much that of the professional writer as the man

[41] M. Dewar, "The Authorship," where these arguments are devel-
oped fully and a contrast is drawn between the *Discourse* and known
views of John Hales, e.g., his dislike of the civil law, his approval of
active lay participation in church affairs, his discouragement of the
manufacture of cloth within the realm, his totally different explanation of the inflationary phenomena of the time, and above all his ad-
herence to the traditional "commonwealth" view that the troubles of
society arose solely from the greed of men for private profit which
should be restrained by law.
[42] M. Dewar, *Sir Thomas Smith*, pp. 50–51.

of affairs. In 1542 when Cambridge University had been divided by sharp and bitter controversy over attempts to introduce the new pronunciation of Greek against the Chancellor's opposition, Smith had taken to his pen and produced a book arguing the case for the new pronunciation.[43] In 1561 when all England was ringing with argument over Elizabeth's duty to marry and the problems involved in her choice, he wrote the "Dialogue on the Queen's Marriage" in a style very similar to the *Discourse* with four characters walking in a garden, freely pursuing their points of view.[44] In 1571 when Elizabeth was reluctant to undertake the schemes of Irish conquest advised by her councillors, he wrote an open letter *"By I. B. Gentleman, etc."* arguing the case for colonizing enterprises in Ireland.[45] It is not surprising therefore to find that he turned to the same technique in 1549. He was cut off from influence at Court and was brooding over the social situation, "the miserable estate, our commonwealth," [46] as he wrote to Cecil in July. He was incensed by the rejection of his advice. Perhaps the *Discourse* was sent to Cecil. The author notes that "it is dangerous to meddle in the King's matters" and stresses that the book was only "between us two to be weighed only and considered and not to be published abroad." Somerset's well-known dislike of criticism no doubt had a lot to do with the early obscurity surrounding the authorship of the *Discourse*. The device of using an imaginary conversation between five characters was a useful convention; it was far less dangerous than an openly expressed viewpoint.[47]

---

[43] See above, *n.* 30.   [44] See above, *n.* 33.   [45] See above, *n.* 35.

[46] Smith to Cecil, July 19, 1549, *Calendar of State Papers, Domestic, 1547–80* (London, 1856), p. 20.

[47] The author admits that this was a deliberately chosen literary device, "that kind of reasoning seems to me best for bolting out of the truth which is used by way of dialogue or colloquy, where reasons be made to and fro as well for the matter intended as against it." Attempts which have been made (e.g., by E. Lamond) to "identify" the "scene of the conversation" and the five characters are simply misleading and quite unnecessary.

Sir Thomas Smith died in 1577, and in 1580 his nephew and heir William Smith took over his uncle's house of Hill Hall, Essex, and promptly began work on his uncle's old papers.[48] The following year the first edition of the *Discourse* appeared and two years later the first edition of the *De Republica Anglorum* which Smith had written in 1565. That William Smith was the "W. S." of the printed 1581 edition seems fairly certain. Lambarde's early manuscript edition has "William Smith" scribbled down as an identification of "W. S." and the "Epistle Dedicatory," added by "W. S." in 1581, gives further clues. "W. S." expresses gratitude for Elizabeth's "late & singular clemency in pardoning certain my undutiful misdemeanor" as William Smith also had cause to do; in 1580 he had aroused her anger by his ill-judged attempt to recover his uncle's inheritance in Ireland.

The nature of the alterations made to the original text for the 1581 edition also point to an identification of "W. S." and William Smith. The 1581 edition differed from the original text as can be seen by comparing it with Lambarde's early copy and our four other known manuscript texts.[49] There was throughout a clumsy attempt to bring the work up-to-date; original references to "nowadays" and "present times" were deleted or altered, and specific price references or comments on the current state of the coinage were modified. These alterations are mostly clumsy and inept, not the work of a skilled writer. There is moreover a casual uncritical acceptance of obviously ridiculous clerical errors in the manuscript from which he was adapting.[50] Two notebooks of William Smith which survive[51] do not reveal any literary talent, and many of their

[48] He copied several items from Sir Thomas' papers with his own comments added in a notebook which also has dated memoranda of his own affairs.

[49] The four MSS are: 1. The Yelverton MS, B.M. Add. MS 48047 ff. 174–227. 2. The Bodleian MS Add. C. 273. 3. The Hatfield MS 269/2. 4. The Albany MS.

[50] See Appendix B.

[51] 1. B.M. Lansdowne MS 210. 2. Essex Record Office D/DSh/Z1.

entries betray a similar slipshod level of accuracy and comprehension. He was however meticulous over one point. Every time there was a reference in the 1549 text to the leading character, the Doctor, as being in orders, William altered this in the printed version to the third person: "Us that be ministers of the church" is changed to "them" and so on.[52] William was somewhat earnest on the subject of religion, and the family was sensitive to a charge that Smith had been in orders which he had cast off for the benefits of office.[53] The published version therefore endeavors to give no hint at all that the author's mouthpiece, the Doctor, was in orders, an attempt which removes much of the vitality from that section of the Third Dialogue in which religion is discussed.

The major change in the printed version was the addition of the brilliant new section mentioned earlier [54] which discussed the impact of the precious metals from the New World on price levels in terms of Bodin's original suggestion.[55] It seems fairly certain that this new section was added not by "W. S." but by the original author. We know that Smith, who was always considered an authority on monetary matters,[56] was familiar with contemporary foreign authors on the subject, and it is very likely that he was acquainted with Bodin's suggestion. We know that in the summer of 1576 he looked over his old manuscripts, revising some of them, and endeavoring to resuscitate books "made in my youth" and since "lost." [57] The brilliance and unquestionable similarity of style of this new section to the rest of the book point very much to the author's own revision. It would certainly have been beyond the range of the "W. S." who found the simple task of updating the book almost beyond his capacity.

---

[52] E. Lamond notes many of these emendations, e.g., *op. cit.*, pp. 131, 139.

[53] M. Dewar, *Sir Thomas Smith*, p. 30.   [54] P. xv.

[55] See above, *nn.* 14, 15.   [56] M. Dewar, "The Authorship."

[57] *Ibid.*, p. 398.

A DISCOURSE OF THE COMMONWEAL
OF THIS REALM OF ENGLAND

A Table of Things Most Notable
Contained in This Book

[1] *Prohemium:* introduction, preface.

Why gentlemen do give over their households.

Why gentlemen do take farms to their hands.

A complaint against sheep.

The Doctor's complaint for men of his sort.

A complaint against learned men.

Why learning should be likely to decay hereafter.

Whether a Commonweal may be well governed without learning.

That the learned have always had the sovereignty over the unlearned.

Whether a man may be wise without learning.

That learning supplies the lack of experience and that experience is the father of wisdom.

The wonderful gifts that we have by learning.

That there is no faculty but is made more consummate by learning.

How Caesar excelled all other captains by reason of his great learning joined with his prowess.

That knowledge in moral philosophy is most necessary for a counselor.

What makes learned men to be few.

That young students be always overhasty in uttering their judgments.

That Pythagoras commanded silence to his disciples for a time.

That Plato commanded that no man ignorant in geometry should enter his school.

What harm may come if they be suffered to judge in things to whom that does not appertain.

That it is not learning sufficient to know tongues and to write.

Why learning should decay.

That every estate finds himself aggrieved.

That merchants can best save themselves in every alteration.

Of our old coin exhausted.

Whether it made any matter of what matter of what metal the coin be made.

What men are most pinched by this same dearth.

That the King's Highness has most loss by this universal
dearth.

What danger should it be to the realm if the King should
want treasure in time of need.

How His Highness cannot have treasure when his subjects
have none.

To what profit the new mint is like.

A recapitulation of the common griefs.

2. DIALOGUE

That it is a marvelous dearth that comes in the time of
plenty.

The occasion of this dearth is laid to the gentlemen.

How from the gentlemen it is laid to the husbandmen.

The gentlemen's excuse and reasonable offer.

The husbandman refuses and puts over the fault to iron-
mongers and clothiers.

If all lands were abated in their rent whether this dearth
would be remedied.

That it were not expedient that strangers should sell their
wares dear and we ours good cheap.

Another offer of the gentleman made to the husbandman.

Whether, if the husbandman were forced to abate the price
of his stuff, this dearth should be then amended.

The strangers will take but money current everywhere for
their wares, that they have over their exchange.

That strangers and all merchants bring things that be best
cheap to them and dearest with us.

What things is of that sort.

He that sells good cheap and buys dear shall not lightly
thrive.

It is not possible to keep our treasure from going forth of
the realm if it be in more estimation elsewhere.

That the dearth rose at neither the gentleman's nor the husbandman's hands.

Permutation of things before coin.

A complaint against sheepmasters.

That enclosures is occasion of desolation and weakening of the power of the realm.

Reasons to defend enclosures.

What kind of enclosures is hurtful.

Whether that that is profitable to one may be profitable to all other if they use the same feat.

Every commodity must be so advanced as it be not prejudicial to other greater commodities.

No man may abuse his own things to the prejudice of the Commonweal.

How enclosures might be remedied without coercion of laws.

That a like restraint of wool should be made as is of corn, or none to be sent over unwrought.

Reasons why the husbandman should not [2] be at liberty as others to sell his wares.

That by breeding the husbandman has most clear gains.

That profit advances all faculties.

That some are to be allured by rewards and some other[s] with straight pains forced in a Commonweal.

The less honor or profit is given to any art the less it shall be frequented.

Profit will make husbandmen more occupied and thereby more plenty and consequently better cheapness of corn.

Whether the King's custom should be diminished by restraint of wool unwrought?

How strangers fetch from us our great commodities for very trifles.

Our delicacy in requiring strangers' wares.

The increase of haberdashers and milliners over they were wont to be.

How the strangers find an easier way to get treasure by things of no value than by any mines of gold or silver.

How strangers find their people with our commodities and [on] our cost.

[2] The copyist's error; the sense of the passage referred to requires "should be at liberty." This is an error common to (Y), (H), and (S). Curiously, (B) inserts the "not" and then crosses it out.

Why strangers may forth [3] wares made by them better than we may the same made here, and yet that it were better for us to buy our own, though they were dearer.

The most durable and universal profit is more to be esteemed than short and particular.

Whether such restraints do touch the leagues made with outward princes.

No league is to be cherished that is not for the Commonweal.

A worthy example to be followed in using of strangers.

What harm comes and may come by alteration of the coin.

That the substance and quantity is esteemed in coin and not the name.

That the necessity of mutual traffic and commodity of exchange made coin to be devised.

Why gold and silver were the stuff most meet for coin to be struck in.

Why gold and silver are esteemed afore all other metals.

Why gold and silver were coined.

Sometime brass, silver, and gold were weighed before coin made.

What loss comes of loss of credence.

What do strangers bring us for our treasure and chief commodities.

How our old coin may be transported and the King and his officers not aware.

We devise the readiest way to drive away our treasure.

Why things within the realm should be so dear.

Some have gains by the alteration of the coin.

Who has loss by the alteration of the coin.

Of excess in apparel.

In peace look for war.

Of excess in building.

How the alteration of the coin is most loss to the King.

Money is called *Nervi bellorum*.

For recovering of our treasure home again.

[3] *Forth:* sell.

Whether all our wool were expedient to be sold over unwrought.

Mysteries are to be increased rather than diminished.

Of three sorts of mysteries.

One brings out our treasure.

Another spends that they get in the same country again.

The third sort brings in treasure and therefore most to be
cherished.

Mysteries do enrich countries that be else barren.

Alliances with strangers are to be purchased and kept.

Whether gendarmes were necessary here as in France.

A less grief would not be helped with a greater sore.

3. DIALOGUE

The common griefs.

The original cause in everything is to be searched for.

Divers sorts of causes there be.

How one thing is cause of the other and that of the third.

The strangers' answer touching the dearth.

That the alteration of the coin should be the very cause of
this dearth and consequently of other griefs.

Either by example or by art anything must be amended.

The remedy to be only by restoring the coin to the old rate
and names.

All the coin being together current must be of equal value
in proportion one toward the other.

Confusion of the metal gives occasion of deceit.

Not only the substance and quantity but also the names of
the pieces of coin must be after the accustomed manner.

That the coin is the common measure.

It is not enough for a man to be paid in like number but also
in like quantity.

It made no matter although some coin were of brass, so it
kept a due proportion of his estimate toward silver and
gold.

What proportion was between silver and gold two thousand
years ago, the same is yet at this day.

How the treasure might be had to reform the coin.

A prince ought to have a great treasure, or else his subjects, against all events.

That that is universally esteemed must not be rejected of any Commonweal that must have traffic with others.

Coin once made of leather but that in time of great need and for a small space.

How the mintners do multiply.

A mintner's rare example.

A case to be provided for if the coin were amended, touching men's rents late enhanced.

How enclosures might be remedied.

Of towns decayed.

The occasion of the decay of our towns.

That art is to be most cherished in a town that brings most to the town.

Towns are enriched with some one trade.

The occasion of the schism in matters of religion.

The faults on the part of the laity.

How this schism might be remedied.

A DISCOURSE OF THE COMMONWEAL
OF THIS REALM OF ENGLAND

The Preface

CONSIDERING the manifold complaints of men touching the decay of this Commonweal that we be in, moved more *decay* at this present than of long time past has been heard, some imputing it to one thing and some to another, albeit I am not of the King's Council to whom the consideration and reformation of the same does chiefly belong, yet, knowing myself to be a member of the same Commonweal and called to be one of the Common House, where such things ought to be treated of, I cannot reckon myself a mere stranger to this matter; no more than a man that were in a ship which were in danger of wreck might say that, because he is not percase the master or pilot of the same, the danger thereof did pertain nothing to him.[†] Therefore, having now some vacation from other business, methought I could not apply my study to any better thing than to make some discourse with myself. First, what things men are most grieved with, then what should be the occasion of the same, and that known, how such griefs may be taken away and the state of the Commonweal reformed again. And albeit you might well say that there be men of greater wit that have the matter in charge than I, yet fools (as the proverb is) sometimes speak to the purpose, and as many heads, so many wits. And therefore princes, though they be never so wise themselves, yea the wiser that they be, the more counselors they will have; for that that one cannot perceive, another shall.

[†] *No man is a stranger in the Commonweal that he is in.*

The gifts of wit be so divers. Some excel in memory, some in invention, some in judgment, some at the first sight ready, and some after long consideration. And though each of these by themselves do not make perfect the thing, yet when every man brings in his gift a mean-witted man may of the whole (the best of every man's devise [1] being gathered together) make as it were a pleasant garland and perfect to adorn his head with.[‡] Therefore I would not only have learned men (whose judgment I would wish to be chiefly esteemed herein) but also merchantmen, husbandmen, and artificers (which in their calling are taken wise) freely suffered, yea and provoked, to tell their advice in this matter; for some points in their feats they may disclose that the wisest in a realm could not [gainsay]. And it is a maxim, or a thing perceived as an infallible verity among all men, that every man is to be credited in that art that he is most exercised in.[§]

Did not Apelles,[2] that excellent painter, consider that when he laid forth his fine image of Venus to be seen of every man that passed by to the intent he (hearing every man's judgment in his own art) might always amend that was amiss in his work; whose censures he allowed, so long as they kept them within their own faculties and took not upon themselves to meddle with another man's art. So percase I may be answered as he was, yet I refuse not that if I pass my compass. But forasmuch as most of this matter contains policy or good government of a Commonweal, being a member of Philosophy Moral wherein I have somewhat studied, I shall be so bold with you (who I doubt not will construe everything to the best) as to utter my poor conceit herein. And since this is between us two to be

[‡] *Of many heads is gathered a perfect counsel.*

[§] *That every man is to be credited in his own art.*

[1] *Devise:* discourse, communication.

[2] Apelles, the celebrated Greek painter, was most admired for his "Aphrodite Anadyomene," here called the "Venus Anadyomene." He was credited with the maxim referred to here *ne sutor supra crepidam*, i.e., "everyman to his own trade."

weighed only and considered and not to be published abroad, though I should herein percase move some things that were openly not to be touched as in such cases of disceptation [3] is requisite, yet, having respect to what end they be spoken, I trust they can offend no man. For hard were it to heal a sore that a man would not have opened to his physician, nor yet of a surfeit that a man would not declare the occasion of. Therefore now, to go to the matter upon boldness of your good acceptance, that kind of reasoning seems to me best for bolting out of the truth which is used by way of dialogue or colloquy, where reasons be made to and fro as well for the matter intended as against it.[||] I thought best to take that way in the discourse of this matter, which is first in recounting the common and universal griefs that men complain on nowadays. Secondly in bolting out the very causes and occasions of the same, and thirdly and finally in devising remedies for all the same.[†] Therefore I will declare unto to you what communication a knight told me was between him and certain other persons of late about this matter, which, because it happened between such persons as were members of every estate that find themselves grieved nowadays and touched all those matters (as methought well), I thought it not meet to be forgotten. The persons were these: a knight, as I said first, a merchantman, a doctor, a husbandman, and a craftsman. The knight rehearsed the communication thus:

[||] *Why the book is made by way of dialogue.*
[†] *The sum of the whole book.*
[3] *Disceptation:* dispute, discussion.

The First Dialogue

KNIGHT. After I and my fellows, the Justices of the Peace of this county, had the other day declared the King's Highness Commission touching enclosures and given the charge to the inquest, I, being both weary of heat of the people and noise of the same, thought to steal to a friend's house of mine in the town which sells wine to the intent to eat a morsel of meat (for I was as then fasting) taking with me an honest husbandman whom for his honesty and good discretion I loved very well. Whither as we were come and had but scant sat down together in a close parlor, there comes one in, a merchantman of that city, a man of good estimation and substance, and requires the said husbandman to go and dine with him. Nay, quoth I, he will not, I trust, now forsake my company though he should fare better with you.

MERCHANT. Then, quoth the merchant, I will send home for a pasty of venison that I have there and for a friend of mine and a neighbor that I had bidden to dinner. And we shall be so bold as to make merry with all here in your company. And as for my guest he is no stranger to you neither and therefore both he of yours and you of his company I trust will be the gladder.

KNIGHT. Who is it?

MERCHANT. Doctor Pandotheus.

KNIGHT. Is he so? On my faith he shall be heartily welcome. For of him we shall have some good communication,
and wise; for he is noted a learned and wise man. And anon
the merchant sent for him and he comes unto us, and withal
an honest man, a capper of the same town, which came to
speak with the said merchant. Then, after salutations had,
as you know the manner is, between me and Master Doctor
and renewing of old acquaintance which had been long
before between us, we sat all down. And when we had eaten
somewhat to satisfy the sharpness of our stomachs, the
Doctor quoth to me.

DOCTOR. On my faith you have yourself and make to
others much ado, you that be Justices of the Peace of every
county; you in sitting upon commissions almost weekly
and they in appearing before you and leaving their husbandry unlooked to at home.

KNIGHT. Surely it is so; yet the King must be served and
the Commonweal. For God and the King have not sent us
the poor living we have but to do service therefore abroad
among our neighbors.

DOCTOR. It is well if you take it so; for nature has grafted
that persuasion in you and all others that follow the clear
light of nature. As learned men have remembered, saying,[‡]
we be not born only to ourselves but partly to the use of
our country, of our parents, of our kinfolk, and partly of
our friends and neighbors.[§] And therefore all good virtues
are grafted in us naturally, whose effects be to do good to
others, wherein shows forth the image of God in man whose
property is ever to do good to others and to distribute his
goodness abroad, like no niggard nor envious thing.[‖] Other
creatures, as they resemble nothing of that godly image, so
they study no common utility of other but only the con-

---

‡ *Plato.*   § *Cicero.*
‖ *That men are not born to themselves only.*

servation of themselves and propagation of their own kind. Wherefore, if we look to be reckoned most unlike them being most vile and like to God being most excellent, let us study to do good to others, not preferring the ease of this carcass which is like the brute beast's but rather the virtues of the mind, wherein we be like God himself. Then said the husbandman,

HUSBANDMAN. For all your pains (meaning by me) and ours also, I would you had never worse commissions in hand than this is. So we had lost more days' work at our husbandry than this.

KNIGHT. Why so?

HUSBANDMAN.† Marry, for these enclosures do undo us all; for they make us to pay dearer for our land that we occupy and causes that we can have no land in manner for our money to put to tillage. All is taken up for pasture, either for sheep or for grazing of cattle. So that I have known of late a dozen plows within less compass than six miles about me laid down within these seven years; and where forty persons had their livings, now one man and his shepherd has all. Which thing is not the least cause of these uproars, for by these enclosures many too many do lack livings and be idle. And therefore for very necessity they are desirous of a change, being in hope to come thereby to somewhat and were assured that, howsoever it befell with them, it can be no harder with them than it was before. Moreover all things are so dear that by their day's wage they are not able to live.

CAPPER.‡ I have well the experience thereof for I am fain to give my journeymen twopence in a day more than I was wont to do and yet they say they cannot sufficiently live thereon. And I know it for truth that the best husband of

† *Complaint of enclosures by husbandmen.*
‡ *Complaint of dearth of victuals by artificers.*

them can save but little at the year's end; and, by reason of such dearth as you speak of, we that are artificers are able to keep but few or no apprentices like as we were wont to do. And therefore this city which was heretofore well inhabited and wealthy (as you know everyone of you) is now for lack of occupiers fallen to great desolation and poverty.

MERCHANTMAN.§ So be the most part of all the towns of England, London only excepted. And not only the good towns are sore decayed in their houses, walls, streets, and other buildings, but also the country in their highways and bridges; for such poverty reigns everywhere that few men have so much to spare as they may give anything to the reparation of such ways, bridges, and other common easements. And albeit there be many things laid down now, which beforetimes were occasions of much expense—as stage plays, interludes, May games, wakes, revels, wagers at shooting, wrestling, running, and throwing the stone or bar, and besides that pardons, pilgrimages, offerings, and many such other things—yet I perceive we be never the wealthier but rather the poorer.‖ Whereof it is long ¹ I cannot well tell; for there is such a general dearth of all things as I never knew the like, not only of things growing within this realm, but also of all other merchandise that we buy from beyond the sea † as silks, wines, oil, wood, madder,² iron, steel, wax, flax, linen cloth, fustians, worsteds, coverlets, carpets, arrases and tapestry, spices of all sorts, and all haberdashery wares, as paper both white and brown, glasses as well drinking and looking as for glazing of windows, pins, needles, knives, daggers, hats, caps, brooches, buttons, and lace. I wot ³ well

§ *Complaint of decay of towns by merchantmen and of all other common easements.*

‖ *Many superfluous charges laid down and yet never the more plenty.*

† *Dearth of outward merchandise.*

¹ *Long or along of:* attributable to, owing to, on account of.

² *Madder:* A dye from a plant. The reddish-colored dye was imported at this time chiefly from France and Holland.

³ *Wot:* know.

all these do cost me more by the third part well than they did but seven years ago. Then all kinds of victuals are as dear or dearer again,‡ and no cause of God's part thereof, as far as I can perceive, for I never saw more plenty of corn, grass, and cattle of all sort than we have at this present and have had, as you know, all these three years past continually, thanked be Our Lord God. If these enclosures were cause thereof or any other thing else, it were pity but they were removed.

KNIGHT.   Since you have plenty of all things of corn and cattle as you say, then it should not seem this dearth should be long of these enclosures. For it is not for scarcity of corn that you have this dearth, for, thanks be to God, corn is good cheap and so has been these three years past continually. That it cannot be the occasion of the dearth of cattle, for enclosure is the thing that nourishes cattle most of any other.§ Yet I confess there is a wonderful dearth of all things, and that do I and all men of my sort feel most grief in, which have no wares to sell or occupation to live by but only our land.‖ For you all three, I mean you my neighbors, the husbandman, and you master merchant, and you goodman capper and all sort of artificers, may save yourselves meetly well; ⁴ forasmuch as all things are dearer than they were, so much do you rise in the price of wares and occupations that you sell again. But we have nothing to sell whereby we might advance the price thereof to countervalue those things that we must buy again.

HUSBANDMAN.   Yes, you raise the price of your lands, take farms also and pastures to your hands which was wont to be poor men's livings,† such as I am, and gentlemen [ought] to live only upon their lands.

‡ *Dearth of all kinds of victuals.*
§ *That enclosure should not be the cause of this dearth.*
‖ *That gentlemen feel most grief by this dearth.*
† *The complaint of craftsmen against gentlemen for taking of farms.*
⁴ *Meetly well:* moderately well, well enough.

MERCHANTMAN AND CAPPER. On my soul you say truth,
quoth the merchantman, and the capper also said no less,
adding thereto that it was never merry with poor craftsmen
since gentlemen became graziers; for they cannot nowadays,
said he, find their apprentices and servants meat and drink
but it cost them almost double as much as it did beforetime.
Wherefore where many of my occupation and others like
heretofore have died rich men and been able to leave honestly behind them for their wives and children and besides
that leave some notable bequest for some good deed, as to
make a bridge, to repair a highway (which things go all to
wrack now everywhere), or to buy some land, either to
help the poor beginners of the occupation, yes, sometimes
they had such superfluity, as they could, over such bequests,
leave another portion to find a priest or to found a chantry
in some parish church. And now we are scant able to live
without debt or to keep any servants at all except it be an
apprentice or two.[‡] And therefore the journeymen, what of
our occupation and what of clothiers and other occupations,
being forced to be without work are the most part of these
rude people that make these uproars abroad, to the great
disquiet not only of the King's Highness but also of his
people. And need as you know has no boot.[5]

MERCHANTMAN. It is true, you know likewise, what other
notable acts men of my occupation have done in this city
before this. You know the hospital at this town's end wherein the freemen decayed [6] are relieved, how it was founded
not very long ago by one of our occupation. And the
custom [7] of this city, how it was redeemed by my father-in-
law of late supposing thereby that the city should be much
relieved which was then in some decay. And yet it decays

[‡] *The craftsman's complaint that he cannot set men to work for the
dearth of victuals.*

[5] *Boot:* remedy, relief.   [6] *Decayed:* reduced to poverty.

[7] *Custom:* The "custom" here refers to the local charges levied on
a community; to "redeem the custom" here means to find the money
from other sources.

still every day more and more. Whereof it should be long I cannot tell.

KNIGHT.[8]   Sir, as I know it is true that you complain not without cause, so it is as true that I and my sort, I mean all gentlemen, have as great, yes, and far greater cause to complain as any of you have. For, as I said, now that the prices of things are so risen of all hands, you may better live after your degree than we; for you may, and do, raise the price of your wares as the price of victuals and other your necessities do rise. And so cannot we so much; for though it be true that of such lands as come to [our] hands, either by purchase or by determination [8] and ending of such terms of years or other estates that I or my ancestor had granted therein in times past, I do either receive a better fine [9] than of old was used or enhance the rent thereof, being forced thereto for the charge of my household that is so increased over that it was, yet in all my lifetime I look not that the third part of my land shall come to my disposition that I may enhance the rent of the same. But it shall be in men's holdings, either by lease or by copy,[10] granted before my time and still continuing and yet like to continue in the same state for the most part during my life and perhaps my sons', so we cannot raise all our wares, as you may yours, and methink it were reason if we did. And by reason that we cannot, so many of us, as you know, that have departed out of the country of late have been driven to give over our houses [II] and to keep either a chamber in London or to wait on the Court uncalled, with a man and a lackey after him

[8] *The gentleman's complaint how he cannot keep like countenance as he was wont to do.*

[II] *Why gentlemen do give over their households.*

[8] *Determination:* the ending of a contract for one reason or another, e.g., the ending of a tenant's contract for such a reason as death without heirs.

[9] *Fine:* the fee paid to the landlord when an entering tenant takes possession.

[10] *By copy:* i.e., copyhold tenure; a tenure according to the custom of the manor recorded "by copy" on the manorial court roll.

where he was wont to keep half a score clean [11] men in his house, and twenty or twenty-four other persons besides, every day in the week. And such of us as do abide in the country still cannot, with two hundred pounds a year, keep that house that we might have done with two hundred marks [12] but sixteen years past. And therefore we are forced either to diminish the third part of our household or to raise the third part of our revenues. For that we cannot so do of our lands that is already in the hands of other men, many of us are forced either to keep a piece of their own lands when they fall in their own possession or to purchase some farm of other men's lands and to store it with sheep or some other cattle to help to make up the decay of their revenues and to maintain their old estate withal.[†] And yet all is little enough.

HUSBANDMAN.[‡]   Yes, those sheep are the cause of all these mischiefs; for they have driven husbandry out of the country by the which was increased before all kind of victuals. And now altogether sheep, sheep, sheep. It was far better when there was not only sheep enough but also oxen, kine, swine, pigs, geese, and capons, eggs, butter, and cheese, yes, and bread, corn, and malt-corn enough besides, reared altogether upon the same land.

DOCTOR.   Then, the Doctor, that had leant on his elbow all this while musing, sat up and said, I perceive by you all there is none of you but have just cause of complaint.

CAPPER.   No, by my faith, except it be you men of the church which travail nothing for your living and yet have enough to live on and have no charge on your hands as we have.

[†] *Why gentlemen do take farms to their own hands.*
[‡] *Complaint against sheep.*
[11] *Clean:* well dressed, properly attired.
[12] *Marks:* from the "mark," a half-pound weight of pure silver; here, the coin worth 13*s.* 4*d.*

DOCTOR.[§]   You say truth indeed. Indeed we have least cause to complain. Yet we know well we be not so plenteous as we have been. The first fruits and tithes are deducted of our livings, yet of the rest we might live well enough if we might have quietness of mind and conscience withal. And albeit we labor not much with our bodies as you say, yet you know we labor with our minds, more to the weakening of the same than by any other bodily exercise we should do. As you may well perceive by our complexions, how wan our color is, how faint and sickly be our bodies, and all for lack of bodily exercise.

CAPPER.[‖]   Marry, I would, if I were of the King's Council, provide for you in that point well a fine,[13] so as you should take no disease for lack of exercise. I would set you to the plow and cart for the devil the good you do with your studies but set men together by the ears, some with this opinion and some with that, some holding this way and some another, and that so stiffly as though the truth must be as they say that have the upper hand in contention. And this contention is also not the least cause of these wild uproars of the people, some holding of the one learning and some of the other. In my mind it made no matter though there were no learned men at all in this realm.

KNIGHT.   God forbid, neighbor, that it should be so! How should the King have counselors then? How should we have Christian religion taught us? How should we know the state of other realms and have conference with them of all countries except it were through learning and by the benefit of letters?

DOCTOR.   Care not therefore good man capper, you shall have few enough of learned men within a while if this world hold on.

[§] *The doctor's complaint for men of his sort.*
[‖] *Complaint against learned men.*
[13] *Well a fine:* a "fine": the ruling given in a court of law. Here the meaning is "a good ruling."

CAPPER.   I mean not but I would have men to learn to write and read, yes, and to learn the languages used in countries about us that we might write our minds to them and them to us, yes, and that we might read the Holy Scriptures in our mother tongue. And as for the preaching, unless you agree better, it made no matter how little we had of it; for of diversity thereof comes those diversities of opinions.

DOCTOR.†   Then you care for no other science at all but the knowledge of tongues and to write and read? And so it appears well that you be not alone of that mind; for nowadays when men send their sons to the universities they suffer them no longer to tarry there than they may have a little of the Latin tongue, and then they will take them away and bestow them to the clerk with some man of law, or some auditor and receiver, or to be a secretary with some great man or other, and so to come to a living whereby the universities be in a manner emptied. And, as I think, will be occasion that this realm within a short space will be made as empty of wise and politic men and consequently barbarous, and, at the last, thrall [14] and subject to other nations whereof we were lords before.

KNIGHT.   God forbid that! We that be gentlemen will with our policy in war provide that we come not in subjection of any other nation, and the stoutness of English hearts will never suffer that though there were no learned men in the realm at all.

DOCTOR.‡   Well, an empire or a kingdom is not so much won or kept by the manhood and force of men as it is by wisdom and policy which is got chiefly by learning. For we see in all kind of government, for the most part, the wiser sort have the sovereignty over the rude and unlearned as in every house the most expert, in every city the wisest

---

† *Why learning should be like to decay hereafter.*
‡ *Whether a Commonweal may be well governed without learning.*
14 *Thrall:* in a state of slavery.

and most sage, and in every Commonweal the most learned are most commonly placed to govern the rest.[s] Yes, among all nations of the world, they that be politic and civil do master the rest though their forces be inferior to the other. The empires of the Greeks and the Romans do that declare, amongst whom, like as learning and wisdom was most esteemed, so their empires were spread widest and longest did continue of all other. And why should you think it more strange that you might now be vanquished than other were beforetime that reckoned themselves as stout men as you be, yes, dwellers of this realm; as the Saxons last were by the Normans, and the Romans by the Saxons afore that, and the Britons by the Romans first of all?

KNIGHT. There may be wise men enough though they be not learned. I have known divers men very wise and politic that knew never a letter in the book and contrariwise as many other learned men that have been very idiots in manner for any worldly policy that they had.

DOCTOR.[ll] I deny not that, but I say that if such wise men as you speak of had had learning to their wit, they had been more excellent, and the other, that you call so simple, had been foolish if they had had no learning at all. Experience in wars makes not every man meet to be a captain, though he travail in it never so long, nor there is no other so apt for the war but with experience and use he is made more perfect. For what makes old men commonly more wise than the young sort but their great experience?

KNIGHT. Yes, experience helps much the wit of man I confess. But what does learning thereto?

DOCTOR. If you grant me that experience does help, then I doubt not but you will grant me anon that learning does

---

[s] *That the learned have always had the sovereignty over the unlearned.*
[ll] *Whether a man may be wise without learning.*

also help much to the increase of wisdom.[†] Let that then be set for a sure ground, that experience does further wisdom and take it as it were the father of wisdom and memory to be the mother. For like as experience does beget wisdom as a father, so memory nourishes it as a mother; for in vain should experience be had if the same were not kept in remembrance. Then if I can show you that both experience and also memory are helped and furthered by learning, then you must needs grant me that learning furthers wit and increases it. You confess the experience of an old man makes him wiser than the young because he saw more things than the other. But an old man sees but only things of his own time and the learned sees not only things of his own time's experience but also that that befell in a great many of his ancestors' times, yes, since the world began. Wherefore he needs must have more experience than the unlearned man of what age soever he be. Then so many cases, as he sees in all that time to have happened, could not be so well remembered of any man as it is kept in memory by writing. And then if the unlearned man once forgets the thing he saw, he never lightly remembers it again whereas the learned has his book always ready to call him to remembrance of that he should else forget. Therefore, as he that lives a hundred years must needs have more experience than he that lives fifty years, so he that sees the chances of the world (as it were in a table painted before him of a thousand years) must needs have greater experience than he that lives but one hundred years. Also he that travels many far countries has more experience than other of like age that never goes out of his native country. So he that is learned, seeing by cosmography, histories, and other learning the right manner and usage of every country in the world, yes, of many more than is possible for one man to travel through, and of these that he travels, much better than he could learn there by small tarrying, must needs have more experience than the

---

[†] *Learning supplies the lack of experience and that experience is the father of wisdom.*

other traveler that is unlearned and consequently more wit, being in capacity and memory, both, else equivalent. And now I am forced to consider the marvelous gifts that we have by learning; [‡] that is, how learning supplies unto man the greatest lack that some writers have complained there to be in mankind, that is the brevity of age and the grossness and heaviness of body. Wherein the first, divers beasts, as harts and many other, and in the last, all birds seem to excel man. For where it is denied man to live above a hundred years or thereabouts, by the benefits of learning he has the commodity of life of a thousand years, yes, two or three thousand years, by reason he sees the events and occurrences of all that time by books. And if he should have lived himself by all that space, how he could have had nothing else to his commodity but that experience of things, the rest had been but travail; which experience he has now by letters and without any travail in manner at all and without the danger that he might himself have been in if he had lived by all that space. As to the other point, that we be not so agile and light as fowls and birds of the air be that we might discur [15] from one place to another, we have the commodity through learning that we should purchase by such peregrinations, as well as we should if we might fly from one country to another like birds and yet with less travail and danger. May we not through cosmography see the situation, temperature, and qualities of every country in the world? Yes, better and with less travail than if we might fly over them ourselves. For that that many others have learned through their travails and dangers they have left to us to be learned with ease and pleasure. Can we not also through the science of astronomy know the course of the planets above and their conjunctions and aspects as certainly as we were among them? And to the knowledge whereof by sight we could never attain though we were as agile as any bird. What is there else profitable or necessary for the conduct

[‡] *The wonderful gifts we have by learning.*
[15] *Discur:* run about.

of man's life here in earth but in learning it is taught more perfectly and more complete than any man can learn only by experience all the days of his life? No, not so much as your feat in war, Sir Knight, no, not your feat, good husbandman, but that either of them are so exactly taught and set forth in learning that neither of you both, though you be never so perfect in the said feats, but might learn many points more than ever you saw before by experience in either of them,§ as you, Sir Knight, in Vegetius ‖ and you, good husbandman, in Columella.†

KNIGHT. I say, again, might we not have them in our English tongue and read them over, though we never went to school?

DOCTOR. Yes, well enough; and yet should you be far from the perfect understanding of them except you had the help of other sciences, that is to say of arithmetic in disposing and ordering of your men and geometry in devising of engines, to win towns and fortresses, and of bridges to pass over; in which things Caesar excelled others, by reason of the learning that he had in those sciences, and did wonderful feats which an unlearned man could never have done.‡ And if you had war on the sea, how could you know toward what coast you be driven without knowledge of the latitude of the place by the pole and the length by other stars? And you (meaning the husbandman), for the perfection of the knowledge of husbandry, had need of some knowledge in astronomy, as under what aspect of the planets and in the entry of what sign by the sun and moon it is time to ear,[18]

§ *That there is no faculty but is made more consummate by learning.*

‖ *Vegetius.*[16]   † *Columella.*[17]

‡ *How Caesar excelled all other captains by reason of his great learning joined with prowess.*

[16] Vegetius was the author of a treatise entitled *Rei militaris instituta* dedicated to the Emperor Valentinian II.

[17] Columella, a Spaniard, wrote *De re rustica*, a twelve-volume work on agriculture.

[18] *Ear:* plow.

to dung, to sow, to reap, to set, to graft, to cut your wood, your timber; yes, to have some judgment of the weather that is like to come for inning [19] of your corn and grass, and housing of your cattle; yes, of some part of your physic,[20] called "veterinaria," whereby you might know the diseases of your beasts and heal them. Then for true measuring of lands had you need of some knowledge in geometry to be a perfect husband. Then for building, what carpenter or mason is so cunning or expert but he might learn more by reading of Vitruvius [21] and other that write of architecture, that is to say of the science of building? And to pass over the sciences of logic and rhetoric, whereof the first travails about the discussion of the true reason from the false, the other about the persuasion of that that is to be set forth to the people as a thing to them profitable and expedient, whereof a good and a perfect counselor might want neither well. Tell me what counsel can be perfect, what Common-weal can be well ordered or saved upright, where none of the rulers or counselors have studied any philosophy, spe-cially the part that teaches of manners? [s] The other part of philosophy I pass over now which teaches of natures and is called physic. What part of the Commonweal is neglected by moral philosophy? Does it not teach first how every man should guide himself honestly? Secondly, how he should guide his family wisely and prophetically, and thirdly it shows how a city or a realm or any other Commonweal should be well ordered and governed both in time of peace and also war. What Commonweal can be without either a governor or counselor that should be expert in this kind of learning? This concerns the point that we now talk of; if men expert in this science were consulted and followed, the Commonweal should be so ordered as few should have cause to complain. Therefore, said Plato, the divine philosopher,[||]

[s] *That knowledge in moral philosophy is most necessary for a coun-selor.*

[||] *Plato.*

[19] *Inning:* harvesting, the "gathering in" of crops.
[20] *Physic:* medicine.
[21] Vitruvius wrote a ten-volume treatise entitled *De architectura.*

that happy is that Commonweal where either the King is a philosopher or whereof a philosopher is the King.

KNIGHT. I had weened [22] before that there had been no other learning in the world but that these men had that be doctors of divinity or of the law or of physic; whereof the first had all his cunning in preaching, the second in matters of the spiritual law, and the third in physic and looking of folks' water that be sick. Marry, you tell me now of many other sciences very necessary for every Commonweal which I never heard of before, but either there be few of these doctors that can skill of them or else they disclose but little of their cunning.

DOCTOR.[†] Of truth, there be too few of them that can skill of these sciences nowadays, and, of those that be, few are esteemed anything the more for their knowledge therein or called for to any council. And therefore others, seeing these sciences nothing esteemed or set by, they fall to those sciences that they see in some price—as to divinity, to the law, and to physic—though they cannot be perfect in none of these without the knowledge of the sciences above touched. And therefore it is ordained by the universities that first men should be bachelors and masters of arts ere they should meddle with divinity. And these arts be the seven liberal sciences: as grammar, logic, rhetoric, arithmetic, geometry, music, and astronomy. And now they skip over them and fall to divinity by and by before they have got or purchased them any judgment through the aforesaid sciences, which makes them to fall to this diversity of opinion that you spoke of now.[‡] For all beginners in every science be very quick and overhasty in giving their judgment of things, as experience teaches every man, and then, when they have uttered and published their judgments and opinions, they will see nothing that will sound contrary to the same but either

† *What makes learned men be so few.*
‡ *Young students be always overhasty in uttering their judgments.*
[22] *Weened:* believed, considered.

they will construe it to their own fantasy or utterly deny it
to be of any authority. Pythagoras to his scholars that came
to learn his profane sciences commanded silence for seven
years that by all that space they should be hearers only and
not reasoners.[§] And in this divine science, every boy that
has not read scripture past half a year shall be suffered not
only to reason and inquire things (for that were tolerable)
but to affirm new and strange interpretations upon the same
never heard of before. What end of opinions can there be
while this is suffered? Also, Plato forbade any man to come
to his school that was ignorant in geometry.[||] And to this
high school of divinity he that knows not his grammar,
much less any other science, shall be admitted at the first, I
say not to learn (for that might be suffered) but to judge,
and there comes in the thing that the same Plato says to be
all only cause sufficient [23] to overthrow a whole Commonweal where it is used; that is, when they take on them the
judgment of things to whom it does not appertain,[†] as youth
of things belonging to old men, children over their fathers,
servants over their masters, and private men over the magistrates. What ship can long be safe from wreck where every
man will take upon him to be a pilot; what house well governed where every servant will be a master or a teacher? I
speak so much of the commendation of learning not only because I heard my friend here, the capper, set little by learning, but also for that I see many nowadays of his opinion
which care nothing for any other knowledge but only that
they may write and read and learn of the tongues, whom I
can resemble well to these men that esteem the bark more
than the tree and the shell more than the kernel.[‡] Wherefore
they seem to take the bright sun from the earth that would

[§] *Pythagoras commanded silence to his disciples for a time.*

[||] *Plato commanded that no man ignorant in geometry should enter his school.*

[†] *What harm may come if they be suffered to judge in things to whom it does not appertain.*

[‡] *That it is not learning sufficient to know the tongues and to write.*

[23] *All only cause sufficient:* i.e., all that is needed.

take away learning from us, for the sun is no more necessary for the increase of all things on earth than is learning for the increase of civility, wisdom, and policy among men. And as much as a reasonable man does excel all other creatures by the gift of reason, so much excels a learned man any other through the polishing and adorning of reason by these sciences.

KNIGHT.   On my faith, I am glad it was my chance to have you in my company at this time. For of a wise man a man may always learn. But methought you said, a while ere, to my neighbor the capper, that we should have learned men few enough within a while if the world did continue. What meant you thereby, and what should be the cause thereof?

DOCTOR.[5]   I showed you already one great cause of the same, that was where I showed you that most men were of that opinion that they thought it learning enough to write and read. Another cause is that they see no preferment ordained for learned men, nor yet any honor or estimation given them, like as has been in times past, but rather the contrary; the more learned the more troubles, losses, and vexations they come unto.

KNIGHT.   How so? God forbid!

DOCTOR.   Marry, have you not seen how many learned men have been put to trouble of late within these twelve or sixteen years and all for declaring their opinions in things that have risen in controversy? Have you not known when one opinion has been set forth and whosoever said against that were put to trouble, and shortly after when the contrary opinion was furthered and set forth were not the other that prospered before put to trouble for saying their mind against this latter opinion? And so neither of both parties escaped business,[24] but either first or last he came to it, of whether side soever he was, except it were some wise fel-

---

[5] *Why learning should decay.*
[24] *Business:* anxiety, trouble.

lows that could change their opinions as the more and stronger part did change theirs. And, what were they that came to these troubles? The most singular fellows of both parts; for there came no other to the concertation [25] of these things but such. Who now, seeing instead of honor and preferment, dishonor and hindrance recompensed for a reward of learning, will other put his child to that science that may bring him no better fruit than this? Or what scholar shall have any courage to study to come to that end? And the rarity of scholars and solitude of the universities do declare this to be truer than any man with speech can declare.

MERCHANTMAN.[||] Then I perceive every man finds himself grieved at this time and no man goes clear as far as I can perceive: the gentleman that he cannot live on his land only as his father did before; the artificer cannot set so many awork by reason all manner of victuals is so dear; the husbandman by reason his land is dearer rented than before. Then we that be merchants pay dearer for everything that comes over the sea by the third part well, and, because they of beyond the sea will not receive our money for their wares as they were glad in times past to do, we are fain to [26] buy English wares for them and that does cost us dearer by the third part, almost the one-half dearer than did beforetime. We pay eight shillings for a yard of cloth that within these ten years we might have bought for four shillings and eightpence. And when we have thus dear bought outlandish ware, then we have not so good vent [27] of them again here as we have had beforetime by reason there be not so many buyers for lack of power, although indeed in such things as we sell we consider the price that we bought them at.

DOCTOR.[†] I doubt not but if any sort of men have licked themselves whole you be the same, for what odds soever

---

[||] *That every estate thinks himself grieved.*
[†] *That merchantmen can best save themselves in every alteration.*
[25] *Concertation:* contention, dispute.
[26] *Fain to:* here, "obliged to."
[27] *Vent:* opportunity for sale; i.e., a market.

there happen to be in exchange of things, you that be merchants can espy it anon. For example, because you touched
somewhat of the coin, as soon as ever you [perceived the
price of that to be enhanced, you by and by] perceiving
what was to be won therein beyond the sea, raked all the
old coin for the most part in the realm and found the means
to have it carried over; so as little is left behind within this
realm of such old coin at this day which in my opinion is a
great cause of this dearth that we have now of all things.*

KNIGHT.   How can that be? What makes that the matter
what sort of coin we have among ourselves so it be current
from one hand to another, yea, if it were made of leather?

DOCTOR.*   Yea, so men commonly say, but the truth is contrary, as not only I could prove by common reason but also
that proof and experience has already declared the same. But
now we do not reason of the causes of these griefs but what
state of men be grieved indeed by this dearth of things.¹¹ And
albeit I hear every man finds himself grieved by it in one
thing or another; yet considering that as many of them as
have wares to sell do enhance as much in the price of things
that they sell as was enhanced before in the price of things
that they must buy—as the merchant, if he buy dear he will
sell dear again, so these artificers as cappers, clothiers, shoemakers, and [farriers] ²⁸ have respect ²⁹ large enough in selling their wares to the price of victuals, wool, and iron which
they buy. I have seen a cap for 14*d.* as good as I can get now
for 2*s.* 6*d.;* of cloth you have heard how the price is risen.
Then a pair of shoes cost me 12*d.* now that I have in my day

---

* *Of our old coin exhausted.*
§ *Whether it makes any matter of what metal the coin be made.*
¹¹ *What men are most pinched by this common dearth.*

²⁸ *Farrier:* one who shoes horses. Only (L) has "farriers"; the other
MSS have "farmores" (H), "fermers" (B), or "fermores" (Y). Farrier is clearly the best reading; this appears to be an occasion when
the Yelverton reading should be overruled.

²⁹ *Have respect:* take note, take into consideration.

bought a better for 6d. Then I can never get a horse shod now under 10d. or 12d. where I have also seen the common price was 6d. for shoeing of a horse round, and 8d. at the most, till now of late. I cannot therefore understand that these men have greatest grief by this common and universal dearth but rather such as have their livings and stipends rated at a certainty, as common laborers at 8d. the day, journeymen of all occupations, servingmen at 40s. the year, and gentlemen whose lands are let out by them or their ancestors either for lives or for term of years so as they cannot enhance the rents thereof, though they would, and yet have the price enhanced to them of everything that they buy. Yea, the King's Highness,† whereof we speak nothing all this while, as he has most of yearly revenues and that certain so has he most loss by this dearth and by the alteration specially of the [coin].[30] For like as a man that had a great number of servants under him, if he would grant that they should pay him pins weekly where before they paid him pence I think he should be most loser himself. So we be all but gatherers for the King's Majesty that be his subjects. We have but everyman a poor living, the clear gains come for the most part to the King's Grace. Now if His Highness do take of us the overplus of our getting in this new coin where he was wont to be paid in other good coin, I report me to you whether that will go as far as the other in the provision of his necessities and of the realm. I think plainly no; for though His Grace might within his realm have things at his own price, as His Grace cannot indeed without great grudge of His Majestie's subjects, yet, since His Majesty must have from beyond the seas many things necessary not only for His Grace's household and ornaments as well of his person and family as of his horses (which perchance might be by His Grace somewhat moderated) but also for the furniture of his wars which by no means can be spared, as: armor of all kind, artillery, anchors, cables, pitch, tar, iron, steel, hand-

† *That the King's Highness has most loss by this universal dearth.*
[30] *Coin:* (Y) has "commons" here, obviously a careless copyist's slip.

guns, gunpowder, and many other things, and artillery more than I can reckon, which His Grace must needs buy from beyond the seas at the price that the stranger will set them at. I pass over the enhancement of the charges of His Grace's household which is common to His Grace with all other noblemen. Therefore I say His Majesty has most loss by this common dearth of all other and not only loss but danger to the realm and all his subjects, if His Grace should want treasure to purchase the said habiliments and necessities for war or to find soldiers in time of need, which passes all the other losses that we spoke of.[‡]

CAPPER. We hear say that the King's Majesty makes up his losses that way by the gains which he has by the mint another way. And if that be too short, he supplies that lack by subsidies and impositions of his subjects so as His Grace can have no lack so long as his subjects have it.

DOCTOR.[§] You say well there. So long as the subjects have it, so it is meet the King should have as long as they have it. But what and they have it not? For they cannot have it when there is no treasure left within the realm. And as touching the mint,[‖] I count the profit much like as if a man would take up his wood by the roots to make the more profit thereof at one time and ever after to lose profit that might grow thereof yearly, or to pull the wool off his sheep by the roots. And as for the subsidies, how can they be large when the subjects have little to depart with? And yet, that way of gathering treasure is not always most safe for the Prince's surety, and we see many times the profits of such subsidies spent in the appeasing of the people that are moved to sedition partly by occasion of the same.

KNIGHT. Now that it was our chance to meet with so wise a man as you be, Master Doctor, I would we did go through

---

‡ *What danger should it be to the realm if the King should want treasure in time of need.*

§ *How His Grace cannot have treasure when his subjects have none.*

‖ *Of what profit the new mint is like.*

with the whole discourse of this matter and like as hereunto we have searched the very sores and griefs that every man feels, so to try out the causes of them; and the causes once known, the remedy of them might be soon apparent. And though we be not the men that can reform them, yet per-case some of us may come in places where we may advertise others of the same and might further and help forward the redress of these things.

DOCTOR. In God's name, I am content to bestow this day to satisfy your pleasure, and though this communication perchance should do no great good, yet it can do no harm, I trust, nor offend any man since it is had between us here apart and in good manner.

KNIGHT. No. What man should be angry with him that were in a house and espied some fault in the beams or rafters of the same and would search the default and certify the goodman of the house thereof, or some other dwelling therein, as well for his own safeguard as for others? But forasmuch as we have thus far proceeded as to the finding out of the griefs †—which as far as I perceive stands in these points: viz., dearth of all things though there be scarcity of nothing, desolation of counties by enclosures, desolation of towns for lack of occupation and crafts, and division of opinions in matters of religion which hale [31] men to and fro and make them to contend one against another—now let us go to the garden under the vine where is a good, fresh, and cold sitting for us in the shadow, where we may proceed further in this matter at leisure, and I will bespeak our sup-per with mine host here that we may all sup together. In God's name, quoth every one of the rest of the company, for we are weary here of sitting so long. And so we all de-parted to the garden.

† *A recapitulation of the common griefs.*
[31] *Hale:* drag, pull, draw.

The Second Dialogue [1]

K<small>NIGHT</small>. When we had walked well, up and down in the said garden a pretty while, I thought long till I had heard more of the said doctor's communication; for he seemed to me a very wise man, not after the common sort of these clerks which can talk nothing but the faculty that they profess as, if they be divines, of divinity; lawyers, of the law; and physicians, of physic only. This man speaks very naturally of everything as a man universally seen that joined good learning with good wit. And therefore I desired him and the rest of our said companions to resort again to the matter that we left at. And first, to discuss and search what should be the causes of the said common and universal dearth of all things, saying to the doctor thus: I marvel much, Master Doctor, what should be the cause of this dearth, seeing all things are (thanks be to God) so plentiful.[‡] There was never more plenty of cattle than there is now of all sorts, and it is scarcity of all things which commonly makes dearth. This is a marvelous dearth that in such plenty comes, contrary to his kind.

D<small>OCTOR</small>. Sir, it is no doubt a thing to be mused upon and worthy the inquisition. Let me hear every man's opinion of you, and then you shall hear mine.

[‡] *That it is a marvelous dearth that comes in time of plenty.*

[1] Two texts (BH) add to the title "wherein the causes or occasions of the said griefs are ensearched." (S) had the clearly stupid error of "are increased."

HUSBANDMAN.[§] I think it is long of you gentlemen that this dearth grows by reason you enhance your rents to such a height as men that live thereon must needs sell dear again or else they were never able to make their rent.

KNIGHT.[‖] And I say it is long of you husbandmen that we are forced to raise our rents by reason we must buy all things so dear that we have of you as corn, cattle, goose, pig, capon, chicken, butter, and eggs. What thing is there of all these things but you sell it now dearer by the one-half than you did within these eight years? I could in this town buy the best pig or goose that I could lay my hands on for 4*d.* which now costs me 8*d.* and a good capon for 3*d.* or 4*d.*, a chicken for a penny, a hen for 2*d.* which now will cost me double the money; it is likewise of great ware as mutton and beef.

HUSBANDMAN. I grant that, but I say you and your sort, men of lands, are the first cause thereof by reason you raise your lands.

KNIGHT.[†] Well, if you and all your sort will agree thereto, that shall be helped. Undertake you that you and your sort will sell us all things at the price that you did twenty years ago, and I doubt not to bring all gentlemen to let unto you their lands at the rent they went at twenty years past. And that the fault is more in you that be husbandmen than in us that be gentlemen appears by this: All the land of the realm, nor yet the one-half, is not enhanced; for some have takings [2] therein, as leases or copyholds not yet expired, which cannot be enhanced though the owners would. And some noblemen and gentlemen there be that when their lands be at their disposition, yet they will enhance nothing above the old rent, so as the most part of the lands of this realm stand yet at the

---

[§] *The occasion of the dearth is laid to the gentlemen.*
[‖] *From the gentlemen it is laid to the husbandmen.*
[†] *The gentlemen's excuse and reasonable offer.*
[2] *Takings:* the profits, receipts, rentals, etc., from land holding.

old rent. And nevertheless there is none of your sort at all
but sell all things they have dearer than they were wont to
do by the one-half. And yet these gentlemen, that do enhance their rents, do not enhance it to the double; though I
confess that some of us, that had lands either given us by the
King's Highness that belonged heretofore to abbeys and
priories and were never surveyed to the uttermost before, or
otherwise descended to us, have enhanced, many of them,
above the old rents. Yet all that amounts not to half the
land of the realm.

DOCTOR.   How say you? quoth the doctor to the husbandman: He says well to you. Will you sell your wares as you
were wont to do, and he will let you have his lands at the
rent you were accustomed to have?

HUSBANDMAN.   When the husbandman had paused a while
he said: If I had the price of everything that I must pay for
besides likewise brought down, I could be content; else not.

DOCTOR.   What things be those?

HUSBANDMAN.[‡]   Marry! Iron for my plows, harrows, and
carts, tar for my sheep, shoes, caps, linen and woolen cloth
for my meinie [3] which, if I should buy nevertheless as dear
as I do now and yet sell my wares good cheap, (though my
rent were thereafter abated) except the other things aforesaid might abate in price together, I could never live.

DOCTOR.   Then I perceive you must have the price of other
things qualified as well as the rent of your lands ere you can
forth your wares good cheap.

HUSBANDMAN.   Yes. But so I think if the land were brought
down that the prices of all things would fall withal.

‡ *The husbandman refuses and puts over the fault to the ironmon-
gers and clothiers.*
³ *Meinie:* household.

DOCTOR.[§]   Grant that all the landlords in this realm would with one assent agree that their land should be in their tenants' hands at the like rent they were twenty years ago, you said before you could not sell your wares as you might twenty years past because of the price that is raised in other things that you must buy. And if you would say that those men should be driven again to sell those wares, that you buy first, better cheap and then you will sell yours thereafter, I pray you how might they be compelled to do so? They be strangers, and not within obedience of our Sovereign Lord, that do sell such wares as iron, tar, flax, and other. Then consider me, if you cannot so compel them, whether it were expedient for us to leave strangers to sell all their commodities dear and we ours good cheap?[||] If it were so, then it were a great enriching of other countries and impoverishing of our own; for they should have much treasure for theirs and have our commodities from us for a very little, except you could devise to make one price of our commodities amongst ourselves and another outwards which I cannot see how it may be.

KNIGHT.[†]   Nay, I will make my neighbor here another reasonable offer if he refuse this. Let my tenant pay me the same coin he was wont to pay twenty years ago as the first agreement was at the first setting forth of my land; and yet I am content to pay him for all things at the price they go now in the coin now current, and I doubt not to bring all other gentlemen to the same agreement.

HUSBANDMAN.   How can I do so? For I must make my rent of such things as I rear upon my taking and of none other thing can I make it, and therefore such money as I receive for my wares, you must take for your rent.

[§] *If all land were abated in the rent, whether this dearth would be remedied.*

[||] *It were not expedient that strangers should sell their wares dear and we ours good cheap.*

[†] *Another offer of the gentleman to the husbandman.*

KNIGHT. Yea, but then let my rent be increased as your payment is increased after the rate, and yet I am content.

HUSBANDMAN. What mean you by that?

KNIGHT. I mean this. You sell that you were wont to sell beforetime for twenty groats,[4] now for thirty; let my rent be increased after that proportion and rate: that is, for every twenty groats of old rent, ten shillings of this new payment, and so as the price of your wares rises; and yet I do but keep my land at the old state.

HUSBANDMAN. My bargain was to pay for my taking but £6 13s. 4d. yearly of rent, and I pay that truly. You can require no more of me.

KNIGHT. I cannot much say against that; but yet I perceive I shall be still a loser by that bargain, though I cannot tell the reason why—but I perceive you sell dear that you live on, and I good cheap that is my living. Help me, Master Doctor, I pray you, for the husbandman drives me to the wall.

DOCTOR. Marry, but methinks, touching the first matter you did reason of, you drove him to his shift; that is, to confess that this dearth rises not at your hands. And though he does defend himself for his payment to you by color of a law, yet he seems to confess thus much, that the law compels you to take little for your land and that there is no law to restrain him but he may sell his wares as dear as he list.[5] It is enough for your purpose that you take in hand to prove that this dearth rose not first at your hand. But whether the price of all things increasing as they do, it were reason you did raise your wares, which is your lands, or to be paid after the old rate when you did let your lands if you be compelled to pay for your provisions after the new rate, we will talk of

---

[4] *Groat:* a small silver coin originally worth about 4d.
[5] *List:* ask, desire.

that hereafter or let that to be considered of other wiser men. But now let us see if the husbandman were forced to sell his things good cheap whether all things should be well then.‡ Put the case thus: that this husbandman should be commanded to sell his wheat at 8*d.* the bushel, rye at 6*d.*, barley at 4*d.*, his pig and goose at 4*d.*, his capon at 4*d.*, his hen at a penny, his chicken at ob,⁶ his wool at a mark the tod,⁷ beef and mutton after the old price as in times past has been. He has then enough to pay his landlord as he had in times past. His landlord again has as much rent as he was wont to have, and the same, when the price is so set, will go as far for the said wares whereof the price be thus set as so much of the old coin paid after the old rent would have done. All this is yet well. Here is yet neither landlord nor tenant grieved. Well, let us go further. The husbandman must buy iron, salt, tar, pitch; and suppose he should be also forced to rear up flax on his own, and that [the] price of cloth, both linen and woolen, and leather were set after the rate. The gentleman must buy wines, spices, silk, armor, glass to glaze his house withal, iron also for tools, weapons, and other instruments necessary, salt, oils, and such other divers things more than I can reckon. Without some whereof they may in no ways live, as iron and salt, for that that is within the realm is not half sufficient for the same—oils, tar, pitch, rosin, whereof we have none at all—and without some other of the said commodities we could live but grossly and barbarously, as without wines, spices, and silks. These must be brought from beyond the seas. Shall we buy them as good cheap after the rate? A man would think yes; for when strangers should see that, with less money than they were wont to take for their wares, they may buy as much of the commodities of this realm as they were wont before with more money, they will be content to take the less money

---

‡ *Whether if the husbandman were forced to abate the price of his stuff, this dearth should be then mended.*

⁶ *Ob:* obolus, a halfpenny.

⁷ *Tod:* a weight used in the wool trade which varied locally but was generally about 28 pounds.

when it goes as far as the more money went before; and so sell their wares as good cheap. As, for an example, where they sell now a yard of velvet for 20s. or 22s. and pay that for a tod of wool, were it not as good for them then to sell their velvet at a mark a yard, so they had a tod of wool for a mark?

KNIGHT. I would think so; for thereby he should be at no more loss than he is now. And so the like reason may serve for iron, wines, salt, spices, oils, pitch, tar, flax, wax, and all other outward commodities.

DOCTOR. If I should then ask you this question, whether they should be compelled by a law to sell their wares so or no, what would you say?

KNIGHT. It makes no matter whether it were so or no, and I think they cannot because they be out of the King's dominion and at liberty whether they will bring any to us or no. But seeing they may have all things here as good cheap at the price they sell, for less money as they had before for the greater price, they will willingly bring their wares and sell them so.

DOCTOR.[8] Thereof I doubt but yet not much; for I think they would sell still at the highest as they do now or bring nothing to us at all. For you must understand they come not always for our commodities but sometimes to sell theirs here, knowing it here to be best vendible, and to buy in other countries other commodities where the same is best cheap; and sometimes to sell in one part of the realm their wares that be there most desired and to go to some other part of the realm for the commodities that be there most abundant and best cheap; or partly of our country, partly of another, and for that purpose coin universally current is most com-

---

[8] *The strangers will take but money current everywhere for their wares that they have over their exchange.*

modious, especially if they intend to bestow it in any other place than where they unload their merchandise. And our coin is not so allowed in other places as it is here; wherefore the stranger should be a great loser if he should take our coin for his wares. He had then lever [8] bring his wares to other places where he might have coin current in all places for it that he might bestow where and when he lists. If they would look but for our wares for theirs, think you that they would not study to bring to us such wares or stuff as should be best cheap with them and most dear with us?

KNIGHT.   Yea, no doubt that is the policy of all merchants.

DOCTOR.   What stuff is that, think you?

KNIGHT.   Marry, glasses of all sorts, painted clothes and papers, oranges, pippins, cherries, perfumed gloves, and such trifles.

DOCTOR.[II]   You say well. They will percase attempt us with such, and such like things are good cheap with them—it costs them but their labor only and their people which else should be idle—yet these things be somewhat, after the price, in other places vendible as well as here. But when we feel the lack of iron, steel, salt, hemp, flax, and such, other such light wares as you speak of will not be desired here but rejected and these other looked for. What other things else will they bring think you?

KNIGHT.   Percase silks, wines, spices, you mean?

DOCTOR.   No, not that, for those be in good price elsewhere.

KNIGHT.   What then should they to have to utter unto us that is best cheap with them and dearest with us?

[II] *That strangers and all merchants bring things that be best cheap to them and dearest to us.*

[8] *Lever:* comparative of "lief"; gladly, rather.

DOCTOR.   I will not tell it, except it be in your ears only; nor it were not expedient it were spoken abroad.

KNIGHT.   I pray you tell me.

DOCTOR.[†]   I know you are a man of trust and of good zeal toward the King's Majesty and his realm. It is, I may tell you, brass; for it goes with them but for brass indeed and therefore good cheap and here it goes a great part for silver and therefore dear with us, and that they will bring unto us.

KNIGHT.   How, in brass pots, pans, and other vessels of brass?

DOCTOR.   No. So no man would take such stuff but for brass indeed.

KNIGHT.   How then? Then the Doctor whispered in my ear and told me:

[DOCTOR] that it was coin made beyond the seas, like in all things to our coin, which they brought over in heaps, and, when they see that esteemed here as silver, they bring that for our commodities; for our wools, our flax, cheeses, butter, cloth, tin, and lead, which thing every man will be glad to sell for the most they can get. And, being offered of strangers more of our own coin than they may get within the country, they will sell them to strangers rather than us with whom the price is set. Then strangers may forth that coin good cheap; for they make it themselves. And the stuff is good cheap that they make it of, and so they will give therefore for our said commodities as much as we will list. Then though they made not such coin themselves, yet seeing they must pay more for our wares or else no man would bring them to them when he may have as much at home of his neighbors, the strangers must need have a consideration of that in the price of the said outward merchandise that

---

† *What thing is of that sort.*

they sell and so hold them dearer. And thus, by the one way they exhaust our chief commodities and give us brass for them, wherewith we cannot buy such like other necessary commodities again as we should want if they were not plenty within our realm. Much like, as Homer said, the exchange that Glaucus made with Diomedes when he gave to this man his gold harness for brazen.‡ By the other way, they must needs be brought to sell their wares dearer to us, and then if this¹⁰ husbandmen and gentlemen and so all other within this realm should be compelled to sell their wares good cheap and yet buy all things dear that come from beyond the seas, I cannot see how they should long prosper; § for I never knew him that bought dear and sold good cheap and use it any long space through.

KNIGHT.   There may be searches made for such coin as you speak of coming in, and punishment devised therefore, and for going forth of victuals also that none shall pass this realm.

DOCTOR.ǁ   There may, but no device imagined so that you be not deceived in both those points, as well in such coin brought in as in victuals brought forth; for many heads will devise many ways to get anything by, and though we be environed with a good pool, that is the sea, yet there is too many posterns to get in and out of unawares of the master. Whosoever has but a pretty house with any family of his own and but one gate to go forth and come in at, and the master of the house never so attentive, yet somewhat shall be purloined forth; much more out of such a large realm as

‡ Glauci et Diomedis permutatio.⁹

§ *He that sells good cheap and buys dear shall not lightly thrive.*

ǁ *It is not possible to keep our treasure from going forth of the realm if it be in more estimation elsewhere.*

⁹ Glaucus was commander of the Lycians in the Trojan War. When he met Diomedes, hero of the Greek army, in battle they abstained from fighting and exchanged arms.

¹⁰ "These," as in the Lambarde MS only, is a better reading but all the other MSS have "this."

this having so many ways and posterns to go forth at and come in. And yet, if strangers should be content to take our wares for theirs, what should let them to advance the price of their wares though ours were good cheap unto them? And then shall we be still losers and they at the winning hand with us, while they sell dear and buy good cheap and consequently enrich themselves and impoverish us. Yet had I lever advance our wares in price as they advance theirs as we do now, though some be losers thereby but yet not so many as should be the other way. And yet what business should there be in making of prices of every trifle; for so it would be if the prices of any one thing be based by commandment. And therefore I cannot perceive that, no more than the dearth has risen at either of your hands both,[†] I mean you gentleman and you good husbandman; for if it rose at either of your hands so it might be remedied likewise at the same by releasing the thing again at either of your hands that was the cause of this dearth. But if either you shall release your rent or you the price of your victuals to the old rate, yet that could not compel strangers to bring down the price of theirs as I have said. And so long as their commodities be dear, it were neither expedient, nor yet could [you] not, though you would, make your commodities good cheap except you can devise a way how to live without them and they without you—which I think impossible—or else to use exchange, ware for ware without coin, as it was before coin was found, as I read in the time of Homer it was and also the civil law does the same affirm.[‡] Which were very cumbersome and would require much carriage of wares up and down, where now by the benefit of coin a man may by those tokens fetch the wares that he lacks afar off without great trouble of carriage, and hard were it readily to find all wares that the one has to pay the other of equal value.

[†] *That the dearth rose at neither the gentleman's hand nor the husbandman's hands.*   [‡] *Permutation of things before coin.*

HUSBANDMAN. Then if neither the gentleman nor I may remedy this matter, at whose hands lies it to be helped then?

DOCTOR. I will tell my mind herein hereafter. But first, let us beat out the cause of this dearth, and therefore let me learn what other thing do you think should be cause thereof.

CAPPER.[§] Marry, these enclosures and great pastures are a great cause of the same whereby men do turn the arable land, being a living for divers poor men beforetime, now [to one man's hand. And where both corn of all sorts and also cattle of all kind were reared beforetimes],[11] now there is nothing but only sheep. And instead of a hundred or two hundred persons that had their livings thereon, now be there but three or four shepherds and the master only that have a living thereof.

DOCTOR.[‖] You touch a matter that is much to be considered. Albeit I take not that to be the only cause of this dearth at this time, but this I think in my mind that if that kind of enclosure do as much increase in twenty years to come as it has done twenty years past, it comes to the great desolation and weakening of the King's strength of this realm which is more to be feared than dearth. And I think it to be the most occasion, of anything you spoke yet, of these wild and unhappy uproars amongst us; for by reason of these enclosures, many of the King's subjects have no ground to live upon as they had beforetime and occupations be not always set awork all alike. And therefore the people

§ *Complaint against sheepmasters.*

‖ *That enclosure is occasion of desolation and weakening the power of the realm.*

11 As stated in the Preface, the words in brackets in this edition correct careless copying errors made by the Yelverton scribe. Here, as in other cases, the words in brackets are found in one or more of the other manuscripts but are omitted in the Yelverton MS. Clearly the scribe's eye slipped from the first "now" to the second "now."

still increasing and their livings diminishing it must needs come to pass that a great part of the people shall be idle and lack livings, and hunger is a bitter thing to bear. Wherefore they must need, when they lack, murmur against them that have plenty and so stir these tumults.

KNIGHT. Experience should seem to prove plainly that enclosures should be profitable and not hurtful to the Commonweal, for we see the counties where most enclosures be are most wealthy as Essex, Kent, Devonshire, and such. And I have heard a civilian once say that it was taken for a maxim in his law this saying, "That which is possessed of many in common is neglected of all," † and experience shows that tenants in common be not so good husbands as when every man has his part in severalty.‡ Also I have heard say that in the most countries beyond the seas they know not what a common ground means.

DOCTOR.§ I mean not of all enclosures, nor yet all commons, but only of such enclosures as turn common arable fields into pastures, and violent enclosures of commons without just recompense of them that have right to common therein. For if land were severally enclosed to the intent to continue husbandry thereon and every man that had right to common had for his portion a piece of the same to himself enclosed, I think no harm but rather good should come thereof, if every man did agree thereto. But yet it would not be suddenly done; for thereby many a thousand cottagers in England, which having no lands to live of their own but their handy labors and some refreshing ¹² upon the said commons, if they were suddenly thrust out from that commodity, might make a great tumult and disorder in the Commonweal. And percase also if men were suffered to enclose their ground under the pretense to keep it still in tillage,

---

† Quod in communi possidetur ab omnibus negligitur.
‡ *Reasons to defend enclosures.*
§ *What kind of enclosures are hurtful.*
¹² *Refreshing:* fresh supplies of food; meat, etc.

within a while after they would turn all to pasture as we see they do now too fast.

KNIGHT.   If they find more profit thereby than otherwise, why should they not?

DOCTOR.[ll]   I can tell why they should not, well enough, for they may not purchase themselves profit by that that may be hurtful to others. But how to bring them that they would not do so is all the matter; for so long as they find more profit by pasture than by tillage, they will still enclose and turn arable lands to pasture.

KNIGHT.   That well may be restrained by laws if it were thought most profitable for the Commonweal, but all men do not agree to that point.

DOCTOR.   I wot well they do not, and therefore it were hard to make a law therein, so many as have profit by that matter resisting it. And if such a law were made yet men studying still their most profit would defraud the law by one mean or another.

KNIGHT.   I have heard oftentimes much reasoning in this matter and some in maintenance of these enclosures would make this reason. Every man is a member of the Commonweal, and that that is profitable to one may be profitable to another if he would exercise the same feat. Therefore that that is profitable to one and so to another may be profitable to all and so to the whole Commonweal. As a great mass of treasure consists of many pence and one penny added to another and so to the third and fourth and so further makes up the great sum so does each man added to another make up the whole body of a Commonweal.

ll *Whether that that is profitable to one may be profitable to all others if he use the same feat.*

DOCTOR. That reason is good, adding somewhat more to it. True it is that that thing which is profitable to each man by himself, so it be not prejudicial to any other, is profitable to the whole Commonweal and not otherwise; or else robbing and stealing which percase is profitable to some men were profitable to the Commonweal which no man will admit. But this feat of enclosing is so that where it is profitable to one man it is prejudicial to many. Therefore I think that reason sufficiently answered.

KNIGHT. Also, they will lay for them another reason; saying, that that is our own commodity should be always advanced as much as might be and these sheep profits is one of the greatest commodities we have. Therefore it ought to be advanced as high as may be.

DOCTOR.[†] I could answer that argument with like reason as I did the other. True it is we ought to advance our own commodities as much as we can, so it be not to the hindrance as much or more of other commodities, or else whereas the breed of conies, deer, or such like is a commodity of this realm, yet if we should all turn our arable ground to nourish that commodity and give up the plow and all other commodities for it, it were a great folly.

KNIGHT. They will say again that all ground be not meet for sheep.

DOCTOR. It is a very ill ground but either it serves to breed sheep or to feed them upon, and if all that is meet either for the one or for the other were turned to the maintenance of sheep and no other thing, where shall we have our other commodities grow?

KNIGHT. All cannot do so, though some do.

---

† *Every commodity must be so advanced so as it be not prejudicial to other great commodities.*

DOCTOR. What should let [13] them all to do that they see some do? Yea, what should better encourage them thereto than to see them that do it become notable rich men by the doing thereof in brief time? And then, if every man should do so, one following the example of another, what should ensue thereof but a mere solitude and utter desolation of the whole realm, furnished only with sheep and shepherds instead of good men? Whereby it might be a prey to the enemies that first would set upon it; for then the sheepmasters and their shepherds could make no resistance to the contrary.

KNIGHT. Who can let men to make their most advantage of that which is their own?

DOCTOR.‡ Yes, marry; men may not abuse their own things to the damage of the Commonweal; yet for all this that I see, it is a thing most necessary to be provided for, yet I cannot perceive it should be the only cause of this dearth. For this enclosure and great grazing, if it were occasion of this dearth of anything, it must be of corn chiefly; and now these two or three years past we had corn good cheap enough, and the dearth that was then most was of cattle, as beef and mutton, and the breed of these are rather increased than diminished by pasture and enclosures.

KNIGHT. Why should men be then so much offended with these enclosures?

DOCTOR. Yes, and not without a great cause; for though these three or four years past, through the great bounty of God, we have had much plenty of corn whereby it has been good cheap, one acre bearing as much corn as two most commonly were wont to do, yet if these years had chanced to be but meanly fruitful of corn, no doubt we should have

‡ *No man may abuse his own thing to the prejudice of the Commonweal.*

[13] *Let:* prevent.

had as great dearth of corn as we had of other things, and then it had been in a manner an undoing of the poor commons. And if hereafter there should chance any barren years of corn to fall, we should be assured to find as great extremity in the price of corn from that it was wont to be as we find now in the price of other victuals; and especially if we have not enough to serve within the realm which may happen hereafter more likely than in times past by reason that there is much land since turned to pasture. For every man will seek where most advantage is, and they see there is more advantage in grazing and breeding than in husbandry and tillage by a great deal. And so long as it is so, the pasture shall ever encroach upon tillage for all the laws that ever can be made to the contrary.

KNIGHT. And how think you that this may be remedied then?

DOCTOR. To make the profit of the plow to be as good, rate for rate, as the profit of the grazier and sheepmaster is.

KNIGHT. How could that be done?

DOCTOR.[§] Marry, two manner of ways, but I fear me the devices shall seem at the first blush so unpleasant unto you, ere you consider it thoroughly, that you will reject them ere you examine them. For we talk now to have things good cheap, and then if I should move a means that should make some things dearer for the time, I should be anon rejected as a man that spoke against every man's purpose.

KNIGHT. Yet say your mind and spare not, and though your reason at the first seem unreasonable, yet we will hear whether you can bring it to any reasonable end.

DOCTOR. Then remember what we have now in hand to treat of: not how the price of things only may be brought

[§] *How enclosures might be remedied without the coercion of laws.*

down, but how these enclosures may be broken up and husbandry more used; of the price of things we shall speak hereafter.

KNIGHT. We will remember well that.

DOCTOR. Then, what makes men to multiply pastures and enclosures gladly?

KNIGHT. Marry, the profit that grows thereby.

DOCTOR. It is very true, and none other thing. Then find the means to do one of these two things that I shall tell you, and you shall make them as glad to exercise tillage as they do now pasture.

KNIGHT. What be these two things?

DOCTOR. Marry, either make as little gains to grow by the pasture as there grows by the tillage or else make that there may grow as much profit by tillage as did before by the pasture. And then I doubt not but tillage shall be as well cherished of every man as pasture.

KNIGHT. And how may that be done?

DOCTOR. Marry, the first way is to make the wool to be of as base price to the breeders thereof as the corn is, and that shall be if you make a like restraint of it for passing over the sea unwrought as you make of corn. You have a law made that no corn shall pass over and it be above a noble the quarter.[14] If it be under, you give free liberty for it to pass over. Let wool be restrained likewise from passing over so long as it is above 13s. 4d. a tod, and when it is under let it

[14] *A noble the quarter:* the noble was a gold coin, a quarter was 8 bushels. "A noble the quarter" was the cutoff price below which corn could be exported without a license.

have free passage; that is one way.[||] Another is to increase the custom of the wool that passes over unwrought, and by that, the price of it shall be based to the breeders and yet the price oversea shall be never the less. But that is increased in the price thereof on strangers shall come to the King's Highness; which is as profitable to the realm as though it came to the breeders and might relieve them of other subsidies. Thus far as touching the bringing down of the price of wool. Now to the enhancing of the price of corn to be as equivalent to the husbandman as wool should be. And that might be brought to pass if you will let it have as free passage oversea at all times as you have now for wool.

MERCHANTMAN. By the first two ways, men would send less wool oversea than they do now, and by that way the King's custom and profits of his staple should be diminished. By your latter way, the price of corn should be much enhanced wherewith men would be much grieved.

DOCTOR. I wot well it would be dear at the first, but I can persuade you that it were reasonable it were so and that the same could be no hindrance to the realm universally but great profit to the same. Then I think you would be content it should be so and as touching the King's custom I will speak afterward.

MERCHANTMAN. I grant if you could show me that.

DOCTOR. I will essay it, albeit the matter be somewhat intricate and, as I showed you before at the first face, would displease many. For they would say, would you make corn dearer than it is? Have we not dearth enough else without that? Nay, I pray you find means to have it better cheap if it may be, it is dear enough already, and such other like reasons would be said. But now, let the husbandman answer

[||] *That like restraint of wool should be made as is of corn or none to be sent over unwrought.*

such men again.† Have not you graziers raised the price of your wools and fells? [15] And you merchantmen, clothiers, and cappers, raised the price of your merchandise and wares over it was wont to be, in manner double? Is it not as good reason then I should raise the price of my corn? What reason is it you should be at large and I to be restrained? Either let us all be restrained together or else let us all be at like liberty. You may sell your wool oversea, your fells, your tallow, your cheese, your butter, your leather—which rises all by grazing—at your pleasure and for the dearest penny you can get for them. And I shall not sell out my corn except it be at 10*d.* the bushel or under. That is as much to say as we that be husbandmen shall not sell our wares except it be for nothing or for so little as we shall not be able to live thereon. Think you if the husbandman here did speak these words that he did not speak them somewhat reasonable?

HUSBANDMAN. I thank you with all my heart; for you have spoken in the matter more than I could do myself and yet nothing but that is true. We felt the harm but we wist [16] not what was the cause thereof. Many of us saw well, years ago, that our profit was but small by the plow, and therefore divers of my neighbors, that had in times past some two, some three, some four plows of their own, have laid down, some of them part and some of them all, their teams and turned either part or all their arable ground to pasture and thereby have waxed very rich men.‡ And every day some of us encloses a[plot] [17] of his ground to pasture, and were it not that our ground lies in the common fields intermingled one with another, I think also our fields had been enclosed of common agreement of all the township long ere this time.

---

† *Reasons why the husbandman should be at like liberty.*
‡ *That by breeding the husbandman has most clear gains.*
[15] *Fells:* hides, skins.   [16] *Wist:* understood.
[17] *Plot:* This word, obviously unclear in the original MS, became a free-for-all for the scribes. (L) has "plucke," (Y) has "plocke," (HB) "plote." (S) abandoned the effort and cautiously wrote "some parte." "Plot" seems to be a reasonably sensible reading.

And to say the very truth, I that enclosed little or nothing of my ground could never be able to make up my lord's rent were it not for a little breed [18] that I have of neat,[19] sheep, swine, geese, and hens that I do rear upon my ground. Whereof, because the price is somewhat round, I make more clear profit than I do of all my corn, and yet I have but a very bare living by reason that many things do belong to husbandry which be now exceedingly chargeable over they were in times past.

CAPPER.   Though this reason here of Master Doctor's does please you well that be husbandmen, yet it pleases us that be artificers nothing at all, which must buy both bread, corn, and malt corn for our penny. And whereas you, Master Doctor, say that it were as good reason that the husbandman should raise the price of his corn and have as free vent of the same oversea as we do and have of our wares, I cannot greatly deny that; but yet I say that every man had need of corn and so they have not of other wares.

DOCTOR.   Therefore the more necessary that the corn is, the more be the men to be cherished that rear it. For if they see there be not so much profit in using the plow as they see in other feats, think you not that they will leave that trade and fall to others that they see more profitable? (As you may perceive by the doings of this honest man's neighbors which have turned their arable land to pasture because they see more profit by pasture than by tillage.) Is it not an old saying in Latin *Honos alit artes*, that is to say, "profit or advancement nourishes every faculty," [s] which saying is so true that it is allowed by the common judgment of all men. We must understand also that all things that should be done in a Commonweal be not to be forced, or to be constrained by the straight penalties of the law, but some so and some

[s] *That profit advances all faculties.* Honos alit artes.
[18] *Breed:* herd.   [19] *Neat:* cattle.

other by allurement and rewards rather.[||] For what law can compel men to be industrious in travail and labor of his body or studious to learn any science or knowledge of the mind? To these things men may be well provoked, encouraged, and allured as if they that be industrious and painful be rewarded well for their pains and be suffered to take gains and wealth as reward of their labors. And so likewise if they that be learned be advanced and honored according to their forwardness in learning, every man will then study either to be industrious in bodily labor or studious in things that pertain to knowledge. Take these rewards from them and go about to compel them by laws thereto, what man will plow or dig the ground or exercise any manual art where is any pain? Or who will adventure overseas for any merchandise? Or use any faculty wherein any peril or danger should be, seeing his reward shall be no more than his that sits still? But you will percase answer me that all their rewards shall not be taken away but part of it. Yet then you must grant me that as if all these rewards were taken from them all these faculties must decay, so if part of that reward be diminished the use of those faculties shall diminish withal after the rate and so they shall be the less occupied, the less they be rewarded and esteemed.[†] But now to our purpose. I think it more necessary to devise a mean how husbandry may be more occupied rather than less, which I cannot perceive how it may be brought to pass but as men do see the more gains therein the gladder they will occupy that feat. And this to be true, that some things in a Commonweal must be forced with pains and some by rewards allured, may appear by that that the wise and politic Senator Tully writes,[‡] saying that it was the words of Solon which was one of the seven wise men of Greece, and of those seven

[||] *That some things are to be allured by reward and some other with straight pains forced in a Commonweal.*

[†] *The less honor or profit is given to any art the less it shall be frequented.*

[‡] *Tullius in* Epist. ad Atticum.

the only man that made laws, that a Commonweal was held up by two things, that is, by reward and pain. Of which words, I gather that men should be provoked to good deeds by rewards and presents and to abstain from ill doings by pains. Think you and [20] husbandmen be not better cherished and provoked than they be to exercise the plow but in process of time so many plows will be laid down, as I fear me there be already, that if an unfruitful year should happen amongst us, as commonly does once in seven years, we should then not only have dearth but also scarcity of corn that we should be driven to seek it from outward parts and pay dear for it.

KNIGHT. How would you have them better cherished to use the plow?

DOCTOR. To let them have more profit by it than they have and liberty to sell it at all times and to all places as freely as men may do other things. But then, no doubt, the price of corn would rise, specially at the first more than at length, yet that price would provoke every man to set the plow in the ground, to husband waste ground, yea, and to turn the land that is now enclosed for pasture to arable; for every man will the gladder follow that wherein they see more gains. And thereby must needs ensue both great plenty of corn within the realm and also much treasure should be brought into the realm by occasion thereof; and, beside that, plenty of all other victuals increased amongst us.

KNIGHT. That would I fain hear you declare how.

DOCTOR.[§] You have heard that by this free vent and sale of corn the husbandman's profit is advanced. Then it is showed that every man naturally will follow that wherein he sees profit, and therefore men will the gladder occupy hus-

[§] *Profit will make husbandmen more occupied and thereby more plenty and consequently better cheap of corn.*
[20] *And:* i.e., if.

bandry. And the more they do occupy husbandry, the more plenty of corn must needs be; and the more plenty there is, thereof the better cheap and also the more will be spared over that that shall suffice for the realm. And then, that may be spared in a good year shall bring us again other corn or else the commodity of other countries necessary for us. Then the more husbandry is occupied, the more universal breed should be of all victuals as of neat, sheep, swine, geese, eggs, butter, and cheese for all these are reared much of corn.

KNIGHT. If men should sell, when a good reasonable year is, all that is overplus when the realm is served, what should we do if a barren year should happen when no store of corn is left of the good year before?

DOCTOR. First, you must consider that men will be sure they will keep enough to serve themselves within the realm ere they sell any forth of the same, and, having liberty to sell at their pleasure, doubt not but they had lever sell their corn 2d. or 4d. in a bushel better cheap within the realm than to be at the charge of carriage and peril of a venture in sending it over and sell it dearer except it be for much more gains. And thus, men being provoked with lucre will keep the more corn, looking for a dear year in the country whereby must needs be greater store. And though they did not so but should sell oversea all that they might spare over that serves the realm when the year is plentiful, yet, by reason that, through the means aforesaid more plows are set at work than would suffice the realm in a plentiful year, if a scarce year should fall after, the corn of so many plows as in a good year would be more than enough, in an unfruitful year at the least would be sufficient, to serve the realm. And so should the realm be served with enough of corn in a scarce year and in a plentiful year with more than enough which might be sold oversea for great treasure or other commodities. Where now is a plentiful year we seek to have but as much as may suffice the realm. Then if a scarce year shall

happen we must needs lack of our own to serve and should
be driven to buy from beyond the sea. And then, if they
were as envious as we be, might they not say when we required any corn of them that, seeing they could get none
from us when we had plenty, why should they let us have
any corn when we have scarcity? Surely common reason
would that one region should help another when it lacks?
And therefore God has ordained that no country should
have all commodities but that that one lacks, another brings
forth, and that that one country lacks this year, another has
plenty thereof commonly that same year, to the intent men
may know that they have need one of another's help and
thereby love and society to grow amongst all men the more.
But here we will do as though we had need of no other
country in the earth but to live all of ourselves and as though
we might make the market of all things as we list ourselves;
for though God is bountiful unto us and sends us many
great commodities, yet we could not live without the commodities of others. And for example, of iron and salt though
we have competently thereof, yet we have not the third
part to suffice the realm; and that can in no wise be spared
if we will occupy husbandry. Then tar, rosin, pitch, oil,
steel, we have none at all; as for wines, spices, linen, cloth,
silks, and collars, though we might live so-so without them,
yet far from any civility should it be. As I deny not but
many things we might have here sufficiently that we buy
now from beyond the seas and many things we might spare
wholly, whereof if time will serve I shall talk more hereafter.
But now to return to the first point I spoke of before to be
one of the means to bring husbandry up, that is, by debasing
the estimation of wool and fells—though I take not that way
to be as good as the other, for I do not allow that mean that
may debase any of our commodities except it be for the enhancing of a better commodity. But if both commodities
may be enhanced together, as by the last device I think they
might be, I allow that way better. Nevertheless, whereas
you, Brother Mercer, showed before that either by restraining of wool and other commodities till they were equivalent
within the realm after the rate of the corn, or by enhancing

the custom of wool and other the said commodities [till the price beside the custom of the said commodities] were brought like to the corn in proportion, the King's Highness custom should be diminished.^{||} I think not so; for the one way, as much as he should have for the more wool at little custom vented over, so much should he have for the less wool at a greater custom vented over. And the other way, as much as His Grace should lose by his custom of wool, so much or more should His Grace win by the custom of cloth made within the realm. But one thing I do note by this latter device, that if they should take place we must do; that is, if we keep within us much of our commodities, we must spare many other things that we have now from beyond the seas. For we must always take heed that we buy no more of strangers than we do sell them; for so we should impoverish ourselves and enrich them. For he were no good husband, that had no other yearly revenues but of his husbandry to live on, that would buy more in the market than he sells again. And that is a point that we might save much by of treasure in this realm if we would, and I marvel no man takes heed to it. What number first of trifles comes hither from beyond the seas that we might either clean spare or else make them within our realm, for the which we either pay inestimable treasure every year or else exchange substantial wares and necessary for them, for the which we might receive great treasure? [†] Of the which sort I mean glasses as well looking as drinking as to glass windows, dials, tables, cards, balls, puppets, penhorns, inkhorns, toothpicks, gloves, knives, daggers, owches,[21] brooches, aglets,[22] buttons of silk and silver, earthen pots, pins, points, hawks' bells,[23] paper both white and brown, and a thousand like things that might either be

---

|| *Whether the King's custom should be diminished by restraint of wool unwrought.*

† *How strangers fetch from us our great commodities for very trifles.*

[21] *Owche* (archaic spelling of *ouch*): a clasp, buckle, or brooch.

[22] *Aglet:* a gold or silver tag or pendant attached to clothes for ornamental purposes.

[23] *Hawks' bells:* small spherical bells fastened to the legs of hawks.

clean spared or else made within the realm sufficient for us. And as for some things, they make of our own commodities and send it us again, whereby they set their people awork and do exhaust much treasure out of the realm. As of our wool they make cloth, caps, and kerseys; [24] of our fells they make Spanish skins, gloves, and girdles; of our tin, salts, spoons, and dishes; of our broken linen cloth and rags, paper both white and brown. What treasure think you goes out of this realm for every of these things? And then for all together, it exceeds my estimation. There is no man can be contented now with any other gloves than is made in France or in Spain; [‡] nor kersey, but it must be of Flanders dye; nor cloth, but French or frizado; [25] nor owche, brooch, nor aglet, but of Venice making or Milan; nor dagger, sword, nor girdle, or knife, but of Spanish making or some outward country; no not as much as a spur, but that is fetched at the Milaners.[26] I have seen within these twenty years when there were of these haberdashers that sell French or Milan caps, glasses, daggers, swords, girdles, and such like, not a dozen in all London. And now, from the Tower to Westminster along, every street is full of them; [§] their shops glitter and shine of glasses, as well looking as drinking, yea, all manner vessels of the same stuff—painted cruses,[27] gay daggers, knives, swords, and girdles—that is able [to] make any temperate man to gaze on them and to buy somewhat though it serve to no purpose necessary. What need they beyond [the] sea to travel to Peru or such far countries, or to try

‡ *Our delicacy in requiring strangers' wares.*

§ *The increase of haberdashers and milliners over they were wont to be.*

[24] *Kersey:* a kind of coarse narrow cloth made from long wool. Broadcloths were fixed at 24 yards long x 2 yards wide, but a kersey was only 18 yards long and a yard and a nail in width.

[25] *Frizado:* woolen fabric with a nap; a fine frieze (see below, *n.* 31).

[26] *Fetched at the Milaners:* bought from a "Milaner," or "Milliner," a vendor of fancy wares and articles of clothing, originally manufactured in Milan.

[27] *Cruses:* pots, jars, drinking vessels.

out the sands of the River Tagus in Spain, Pactolus in Asia, and Ganges in India, to get amongst them, after much labor, small sparks of gold or to dig the deep bowels of the earth for the mine of silver or gold when they can of vile clay, not far sought for, and of [pebble] [28] stones and fern roots make good gold and silver more than a great many of silver and gold mines would make? ‖ I think not so little as a hundred thousand pounds a year is fetched of our treasure for things of no value of themselves but only to the workers of the same which are set awork all on our charges. What grossness of wit be we of that see it and suffer such a continual spoil to be made of our goods and treasure by such means. And specially, that will suffer our own commodities to go and set strangers awork and then to buy them again at their hand; as of our wool they make and dye kerseys, frizados, broadcloths, and caps beyond the seas and bring them hither to be sold again.† Wherein note, I pray you, what they do: They make us pay at the end for our own stuff again for the strangers' custom, for their own workmanship and colors, and lastly for the second custom in the return of the wares into the realm again. Whereas, by working the same within the realm, our own men should be set awork at the charges of strangers; the custom should be borne all by strangers to the King, and the clear gains remain all within the realm.

KNIGHT.   If you weigh such things and other which goes oversea yearly from us for the same, you speak too little by as much again. But one thing I have marked, that albeit it is true, that though strangers buy their wool dear and pay twice custom, that is, both at going out of the wool and when it returns in clothes and caps, yet the same shall be

‖ *How the strangers find an easier way to get treasure by things of no value than by any mines of gold or silver.*

† *How strangers found their people with our commodities and on our costs.*

[28] *Pebble:* This must have been a totally obscure word in the original text. (L) has "pryble," (HB) "peoble," (Y) has "pryple." "Pebble" seems the most hopeful modern reading.

better cheap than that is made within the realm, whereof that should be long, I would fain know.

DOCTOR.[‡]   The Doctor answered again: Whether it be long of our sloth, or of our chargeable fare, or of our idleness which we Englishmen percase use more than other nations, I know not; yet it were better for us to pay more to our own people for these wares than less to strangers, for how little gains soever goes over it is lost to us clear, but how much soever the gains is that go from one of us to another it is all saved within the realm. And a like reason, as you make now, I heard once a bookbinder make me when I asked him why we had not white and brown paper made within the realm as well as they had made beyond the sea. Then he answered me that there was paper made awhile within the realm. At the last, the man perceived, that made it, that he could not forth his paper as good cheap as that came from beyond the seas and so he was forced to lay down making of paper. And no blame on the man; for men would give never the more for his paper because it was made here, but I would either have the paper stayed from coming in or so burdened with custom that by the time it came hither our men might forth their paper better cheap than strangers might do theirs, the custom considered.

KNIGHT.   Marry, there you speak a matter that the King's authority would not agree unto; for if such ware were all made within the realm, then the King's custom should be less by reason that little or no such wares should come from beyond the seas.

DOCTOR.[§]   Yet if the King's attorney did regard as well the profit that should come after, as that is present before the

---

[‡] *Why strangers may forth wares made by them better than we may the same made here and yet that it were better for us to buy our own though they were dearer.*

[§] *The most durable and most universal profit is most to be esteemed than short and particular.*

eyes, he would agree to this well enough; for by this means, inestimable treasure should be saved within this realm. And then it could not grow to the profit of the subjects but it must needs grow also to the profit of the King. And in my opinion, they do not best provide for His Grace's profit that procure only a present commodity but rather a commodity that may endure the longest without grief of his subjects.

KNIGHT. You would have a law made that no such ware should be brought from beyond the sea to be sold here of such things as could be made here as well as there?

DOCTOR. Yea, forsooth, so I would wish.

KNIGHT.^{ll} I was once in the parliament when such a thing was moved, but only for caps, that none made beyond the seas should be sold within the realm. And then it was answered by a great wise man that it was to be feared lest it touched the league made between the King's Highness and some foreign prince. What think you then would have been said if you would have moved a law to be made that nothing made of our wool, or tin, or lead, or hides beyond the sea should have been sold here?

DOCTOR. I cannot tell whether that should touch the league or not, nor whether any such league be, and I say to you that I think it a marvelous league that should let us to make laws to bind our own subjects that might be profitable unto them. And if there were any such league, I had lever it were broken than kept, which being broken should do us good and being kept should do us harm. And I suppose that when we enter any league the same is meant to be for our wealth and not for our hindrance. Wherefore that league would not be esteemed that might hinder our Commonweal.[†]

---

^{ll} *Whether such restraint do touch the leagues with outward princes.*
[†] *That no league is to be cherished that is not for the Commonweal.*

KNIGHT. What, and they would make a like law beyond the sea that wares made in this realm should not be sold there? —as they made of late when we devised a law that no wines should be carried hither in strangers' bottoms.[29]

DOCTOR. Yet should they be forced rather to dissolve their law than we ours; for our stuff is necessary for them that is made here as cloth, leather, tallow, beer, butter, cheese, pewter vessel, and such. Theirs be to us more to serve pleasure than necessity as tables, cards, perfumed gloves, glasses, galley pots, dials,[30] oranges, pippins, and cherries; yea, their chief commodities might be best spared of us than retained of them without, as wines, silks, spices, iron, and salt. I would to God we would follow but the example of a poor haven town that I know did of late here in the Marches of Wales, called Carmarthen.† When there came a certain vessel thither out of England, all laden with apples which before-times was wont to bring them good corn, the town commanded that none should buy the said apples upon a great pain, and so the boat stood so long in the haven without sale or vent until the apples were putrified and lost. And when the owner demanded of the bailiff of the town why he had stayed his sale and vent, the bailiff answered again that the said vessel came thither to fetch the best wares they had in the country as friezes,[31] broadcloths, and wool and instead thereof he should leave in the country but apples and that should be spent and wasted in less than a week. And said, bring to us corn or malt as you were wont to do, whereof the country has need, and you shall be welcome at all times and you shall have free vent and sale thereof in our port. Think you the great cities—London, Southampton, Bristol, Chester, and others—might not learn a good lesson of this poor Welsh town in this doing? Might they not say, when

---

† *A worthy example to be followed in using of strangers.*

[29] *Bottoms:* ship bottoms or holds; i.e., here, any foreign ships.

[30] *Dials:* timepieces of any kind.

[31] *Frieze:* a kind of coarse woolen cloth with a nap, usually on one side only.

ships full of oranges, pippins, or cherries come in, that if they would again take plums, damsons, and strawberries for them they should have free exchange? And when they bring in glasses, puppets, rattles, and such things, they should have like trifles for them, if any such were to be had within this realm as there be not. But if they come for their wools, for their clothes, kerseys, corn, tin, lead, yea, their gold and silver and such substantial and necessary things, let them bring in again flax, tar, oil, fish, and such like and not to use them as men do little children, give them an apple for the best jewel that they have about them. And thus we are impoverished of our treasure and chief commodity and cannot perceive it, such is the fineness of strangers' wits and the grossness of ours. Yet it were more tolerable if we did no more but cherish their devices that be strangers'; but we do nowadays devise ourselves many other ways to impoverish ourselves and to exhaust our treasure. And now I must come to that thing [s] that you, Brother Merchant, touched before which I take to be the chief cause of all this dearth of things and of the manifest impoverishment of this realm, and might in brief time be the destruction of the same if it were not the rather remedied; that is, the debasing or rather corrupting of our coin and treasure, whereby we have devised a way for strangers not only to buy our gold and silver for brass and to exhaust this realm of treasure but also to buy our chief commodities in manner for naught. Yet it was thought this should have been a mean not only to bring our treasure home but to bring much of theirs; but the experience has so plainly declared the contrary, so as it were but a very dullard's part now to be in any doubt thereof.

KNIGHT. Forsooth, such a dullard am I indeed that cannot perceive what hindrance it should be to the realm to have this metal more than that for our coin, seeing the coin is but a token to go from man to man. And since it is stricken with

---

[s] *Of the coin, what harm comes and may come of the alteration of it.*

the King's seal to be current, what makes it the matter what metal it be of, yea, though it were but leather or paper?

DOCTOR.   You say but as most sort of men do say, and yet they be far wide from the truth as men that do not consider the thing groundly. For by that reason, God would never send dearth amongst us but the King might quickly remedy it; as, if corn were at a crown the bushel, the King might provide crowns enough for himself, and also his subjects, made of brass to pay for the same. And so to make it as easy for him and his subjects to pay a crown of such metal for a bushel as it should be for them now to pay a penny for the same. And as the price of corn does rise, the King might raise the estimation of his coin after the rate and so keep the corn always at one estate in deed, though in name it should seem to rise. As for example, suppose wheat this year to be at a groat a bushel and the next year at two groats, the King might cause the groat to be called 8*d.*, and if the bushel rose to 12*d.*, he might raise the estate of the groat to 12*d.* And so, whether it were by making of coin of other metals than be of price received amongst all men or by enhancing the price of the old coin made in metal of estimation, the King might, if your reason were true, always keep not only corn but also all other victuals and necessaries for man's life always at one price in deed though in term they should vary. But you may see daily by experience the contrary hereunto; for when God sends dearth, either of corn or of other things, there is neither Emperor nor King can help it, which they would gladly do, if they might, as well for their own ease as for their subjects'. And might soon do it if your reason before touched might take place; that is, if either they might make coin of what estimation they would of vile metals or else enhance the value of coins made in metals of price to what sum they would.ⁱⁱ Yet a man at the

---

ⁱⁱ *That the substance and quantity is esteemed in coin and not in the name.*

first blush would think that a King within this realm might do this easily and make what coin he would to be current and of what estimation it pleased him. But he that so thinks marks but the terms and not the things that are understood by them. As if a man made no difference between six groats that made an ounce of silver and twelve groats that made in all but an ounce of silver; by the groat of the first sort the sixth part of an ounce of silver and by a groat of the other sort is the twelfth part of an ounce of silver understood. And so there must be as much difference between the one groat and the other as is between two and one, the whole thing and the half; though either or both be called but under one name, that is a groat. We must consider, though gold and silver be metals commonly wherein the coin is struck to be the tokens for exchange of things between man and man, yet [it] is the wares that are necessary for man's use that are exchanged, indeed under the outward name of the coin, and it is the rarity or plenty of such wares that makes the price thereof base or higher. And because that it were very cumbersome and chargeable to carry so much of the wares that we have abundance of to exchange for the wares that we want always—both for the weights of our wares and also for that they could not be carried so far without perishing of the same, nor proportioned so even as there should be always neither more nor less brought for our wares than were equivalent with the other wares that we receive [†]—therefore were the metals of gold and silver devised as wares of so little weight, most in value, and least cumbersome to carry, and least subject to detriment or hurt in the carriage thereof, and may be cut and divided in most pieces and portions without any loss, as the mean wares to exchange all other wares by.[‡] And if the thing were to be new devised, necessity would cause us to devise the same way again. For put the case there were

[†] *Aristotle* lib. 5 Ethicorum.
[‡] *That the necessity of mutual traffic and commodity of exchange made coin to be devised.*

no use of money amongst us but only exchange of wares for wares as sometimes I do read have been.[§] We might at a time have such plenty of things in our realm, as for example of corn, wool, and fells, cheese and butter, that over so much as we should vent out for other commodities as were sufficient for us there should remain with us such great store that spend it we could not in our need nor keep them long without perishing. Would we not be glad to exchange that abundance of things that could not abide the long keeping; which we might exchange again for such wares as I rehearsed, or any other as necessary when scarcity of the same should happen amongst us? Yea, verily. And that we would study to have in that exchange such wares as would go in least room and continue longest without perishing and be carried to and fro with least charge and be most current at all times and at all places. Is not gold and silver the things that be most of that sort?[ǁ] I mean most of value, most light to be carried, longest able to abide the keeping, aptest to receive any form or mark, and most current in all places, and most easily received into many pieces without loss of the stuff. In some of these points I confess precious stones do excel silver or yet gold, as in value and lightness of carriage; but then they may not be divided without perishing of the substance, nor put again together after they be once divided, nor many of them abide so many dangers without perishing of the matter, nor yet receive any stamp or mark easily, nor be so universally esteemed. Therefore they be not so meet for instruments of exchange as silver and gold be, or else they for their price and lightness of carriage might be. And because gold and silver have all these commodities in them, they are chosen by a common assent of all the world, that is known to be of any civility,[†] to be the instruments of exchange to measure all

[§] *Homer ff*. de cont. empt. et vend. lib. primo.

[ǁ] *Why gold and silver were stuff most meet for coin to be struck in.*

[†] Publica mensura *Aristot.* 5 Eth.

things by, most apt to be either carried far or kept in store, to receive for things whereof we have abundance, and to purchase by them again other things which we lack when and where we have most need. As for example, if there were no coin current but the exchange of things as I said sometime there was, set this case; that a man had as much corn in one year as he could not well spend in his house in four years after and perceived that he might not keep it so long or till a dear or scarce year should come, and if he did, much of it should perish or all. Were it not wisdom then for him to exchange the overplus of that corn for some other ware that might be longer kept without danger of waste or diminishing, by the which he might at all times have either corn again at his need or some other necessary thing? Yes, no doubt if there were no use of silver or gold, he would have tin, brass, or lead, or such other like thing that would abide the keeping with less detriment and would desire to have that thing most that were in least weight, most in value, and in least danger of wearing or perishing, and most universally received; wherein gold and silver excels all other metals.

KNIGHT. What makes these metals to be of more value than another?

DOCTOR. No doubt their excellency above all other metals, both in pleasure and use partly, and partly the rarity of them.

KNIGHT. What be those qualities? If you praise the gold for his weight and pliability, lead does excel it in these points. If you commend his color, silver, by any man's judgment, whose color resembles the daylight for clearness, passes him; and heralds prefer it in arms because it is farthest off seen in the field nor never seems other color but his own be it never so far off, where all other shall seem black far off and so lose the strength of their own.

DOCTOR.† As much as the lead approaches the gold in that point I speak of, weight and pliability, it is cast behind it in other qualities far more commendable. And so in color it passes silver by some other men's judgments because it resembles the colors of the celestial bodies, as the sun and stars, being the most excellent things that come under the view of the bodily senses of man, or it is equivalent to it. In arms, I know not how it is esteemed. Well, I wot, princes blaze their arms most with that color, whether it be for excellence of the same or for that they love the metal it is made of so well, I cannot tell. But now to esteem their other qualities: gold is never wasted nor consumed by fire, yea, the more it is burned the purer it is, which you can say of no other metal. Then it wears least by occupying and fouls not the thing it touches as silver does—with whom you may draw lines which is a declaration that the stuff falls away, albeit writers do marvel that it should draw so black a line being of that brightness and color itself. Then there is no rust nor scurf [32] that diminish the goodness or wastes the substances of gold. It abides the fretting liquors of salt and vinegar without danger, which wears any other thing. It needs no fire or it be made gold as other require, it is gold as soon as it is found. It is drawn without wool. It is easily spread in leaves of a marvelous thinness; you may adorn or gild all other metals with it, yea, stones and timber. It is also nothing inferior in commodity of making vessels or other instruments to silver but rather purer, cleaner, and more sweet to keep any liquor in. Next him, approaches silver in commendations as in cleanness, beauty, sweetness, and brightness. And it serves not only to make vessels and other instruments but it is also spun, but not without wool as gold may be—though they could not do that aforetime but with gold only as I have heard vestures were made only of gold then and now of late of this silver; being spun with silk and gilded, they counterfeit the old excess of cloth of

† *Why gold and silver are esteemed before all other metals.*

[32] *Scurf:* deposit, encrustation.

gold and tissue. Now to speak of other metals, you see
what uses they serve for which if those were away should
be more esteemed. Then I told you the rarity commends
the same metals of gold and silver, yet more than this; for
as they do excel in qualities so Dame Nature seems to have
laid them up in a farther ward than her other gifts to shew
us that all fair things be rare and that the fairest things, as
they be hardest to be attained, so they be most to be esteemed. As Erasmus says well, where anything were as rare
as silver, it should be as dear as silver, and not without cause.
Who would glaze a window with silver so as he might keep
out the injury of the weather and yet nevertheless receive
the commodity of the light through the same to his house as
with glass he might? And so I might commend other things
for their use before gold and silver; as iron and steel with
whom you may make better tools for many necessary uses
than with gold or silver. But for the uses that we talk of,
silver and gold do clearly excel all other metals. I pass over
that matter. Thus I have shewn reason why these metals of
gold and silver are grown in estimation above others.

KNIGHT.[§] Why do kings and princes strike these metals
and other with a coin but because they would have that
coin, of what value soever it be, to bear the state that the
coin pretends; which they did in vain if they could make
the metal that bears that to be neither better nor worse in
estimation? Then I had as lever have small gads [33] or plates
of silver and gold without any coin at all to go abroad
from man to man for exchange.

DOCTOR.[‖] Surely the time was so even amongst the Romans
when neither brass, silver, nor gold was coined but were
esteemed only by the weight. And therefore to this day remains these vocables of coin as *libra, pondo, dipondium, as,*

[§] *Why silver and gold were coined.*
[‖] *Plini lib. 33 Cap. 3. Sometime brass, silver, and gold were weighed
before coin made.* Inst. de test. ord. 7.
[33] *Gads:* small plates of iron or steel.

solidus, dinarius, vocables of weight that afterward were
given to coins pretending the same weight; also the common officers that weighed these rude metals were called
libripendes, whereof we have mention in civil law. But because in great traffic and assembly of buyers and sellers it
was tedious to tarry for the weighing of these metals and
trying, it was thought good that the prince should strike
these metals with several marks, for the variety of the
weights they were, to assure the receiver the same to be
no less than the weight it pretended. As for plainer example,
they struck the pound weight with the mark of the pound,
[and the ounce with the mark of the ounce], and so after
the variety of the weights of other pieces, variable marks.
Whereby began the names of coins, so that the people
needed not to be troubled with weighing and trying of
every piece, being assured by the mark printed that every
piece contained the weight that was signified by the mark
set on every one. The princes' credit was then such among
their subjects as they doubted nothing therein. As soon as
they attempted to do otherwise, that is, to mark the half
pound with the mark of the pound and the half ounce with
the mark of the ounce, awhile their credit made those coins
current, as I read amongst the Romans practiced more than
once; † but, as soon as it was espied, the two pieces of half
pound went no further than the one piece of a whole pound
went before, and at length as much as they won at the first
they lost at the last in payment of their rents, customs, and
censes.³⁴ And so the nearer East, the further from West, and
consequently they lost their credit; much like as I have
known certain towns in England to have done which were
wont to make their cloths of a certain breadth and length
and so set their seals to the same. While they kept the rate
truly, strangers did but look on the seal and received their
wares, whereby those towns had great vent of their cloth
and consequently prospered very well. Afterward, some in

† *What loss comes of loss of credence.*

³⁴ *Censes:* taxes levied in early Rome on a property valuation of
people's estates.

those towns, not content with reasonable gains and continually desiring more, devised cloths of less length, breadth, and goodness than they were wont to be and yet by the commendation of the seal to have as much money for the same as they had before for good cloths. And for a time they got much and so abased the credit of their predecessors to their singular lucre; which was recompensed with the loss of their posterity, for after these cloths were found faulty, for all their seals, they were not only never the better trusted but much less for their seal. Yea, though their cloths were well-made; for when their falsehood and untruth was espied, then no man would buy their cloths till they were searched and unfolded, regarding nothing the seal. And yet, because they found them untrue in some part, they mistrusted them in other and so would give less for those cloths than for any other like, having no seals to the same; whereby the credit of the said towns was lost and the towns utterly decayed. Do you not see that our coin is discredited already, especially amongst strangers which before desired to serve us before all other nations at our needs for the goodness of our coin? And now they let us have nothing from them but only for our commodities as wool, fells, tallows, butter, cheese, tin, and lead.[‡] And where beforetime they were wont to bring us for the same either good gold or silver or else as necessary commodities again, now they send us other such trifles as I spoke of before—as glasses, galley pots, tennis balls, papers, girdles, brooches, owches, buttons, dials, or such like wares that stand them in no charge or use—or else, if it be true that I have heard and as I told you in your ear before, they send us brass for our treasures of gold and silver and for our said commodities. I warrant you, you see no gold nor silver brought over unto us as it was heretofore used, and no marvel. To what purpose should they bring silver or gold hither whereas the same is not esteemed? Therefore I have heard say for a truth, and I believe it the rather to be true because it is likely, that since our coin has been debased

---

[‡] *What do strangers send us for our treasure and chief commodities.*

and altered, strangers have counterfeited our coin and found the means to have great masses of that transported hither, and here uttered it, as well for our old gold and silver as for our chief commodity; which thing I report me unto you what inconvenience it may bring the King's Highness and this realm unto if it be suffered in brief time.

KNIGHT.   There be searchers that may let this matter well enough if it be true, both for staying of such false coin to come in and of our old coin to go forth.

DOCTOR.[§]   I said so to the man that told me the same tale that I told you even now, and he answered me there were many ways to deceive the searchers, if they were never so true, as by putting of the said coin in their ship's ballast or in some vessels of wine or other liquor transported either unto us or from us. Then every port or creek in the realm has not searchers, and if they had, they be not such saints as would not be corrupted for money. Besides this, have you not made proclamations that your old coin, specially of gold, should not be current here above such a price? Is not that the readiest way to drive away our gold from us, as everything will go where it is most esteemed and therefore our treasure goes over in heaps? [‖]

KNIGHT.   I believe well that these be means to exhaust our old treasure from us, which we have recited, but how it should make everything so dear amongst ourselves, as you say it does, I cannot yet perceive the reason.

DOCTOR.   Why do you not perceive that by reason hereof you pay dearer for everything that we have from beyond the seas than we were wont to do?

KNIGHT.   Yes, that cannot be denied.

[§] *How our old coin may be transported and the King nor his officers not aware.*

[‖] *We devise the readiest way to drive away our treasure.*

DOCTOR. By how much, think you?

KNIGHT. By the third part well in all manner of things.

DOCTOR. Then must not they that buy dear, sell dear again their wares?

KNIGHT. That is true if they intend to thrive; for he that sells good cheap and buys dear shall never thrive.

DOCTOR.† Then you have yourself declared the reason why things within the realm be so dear; for we must buy dear all things brought from beyond the seas and therefore we must sell again as dear our things or else we should make ill bargains for ourselves. And though that reason makes it plain, yet the experience of the thing makes it plainer. For where you said that everything brought from beyond the sea is commonly dearer by the third part than it was, do you not see the same proportion raised in our wares, if it be not more, yea, in the old coin itself? Is not the angel [35] that was before but twenty groats now at thirty and so all other old coin after the same rate? But I think there is no more silver given in the thirty groat now than was before in the twenty groat, if it be so much. And so I think, setting our coin apart, that we shall have as much silk, wines, or oils from beyond the seas for our tod of wool now as we might have had before the alteration of this coin.

MERCHANTMAN. Then I would undertake to serve you so.

KNIGHT. What loss have we by this when we sell our commodities as dear as we buy others?

DOCTOR. I grant to one sort of men I count it no loss, yea, to some other, gains more than any loss; but yet to some

† *Why things within the realm be so dear.*

[35] *Angel:* a gold coin with a device of the Archangel Michael on it, worth at this period about 10*s.*

other sort a greater loss than it is profit to the other, yea, generally, to the utter impoverishing of the realm and weakening of the King's Majesties power exceedingly.

KNIGHT. I pray you, tell me what be those sorts that you mean, and first of those that you think have no loss thereby?

DOCTOR. I mean all those that live by buying and selling; for as they buy dear so they sell thereafter.

KNIGHT. What is the next sort that you say wins by it?

DOCTOR.[‡] Marry, all such as have takings or farms in their manurance [36] at the old rent for where they pay after the old rate, they sell after the new; that is, they pay for their land good cheap and sell all things growing thereof dear.

KNIGHT. What sort is that which you said had greater loss thereby than those men had profit?

DOCTOR. It is all noblemen, gentlemen, and all other that live either by a stinted rent or stipend, or do not manner [37] the ground, or do occupy no buying or selling.

KNIGHT. I pray you, peruse these sorts as you did the other, one by one, by course.

DOCTOR.[§] I will gladly. First the noble and gentlemen live for the most on the yearly revenues of their lands and fees given them of the King. Then you know he that may spend now by such revenues and fees £300 a year may not keep no better port than his father or any other before him that could spend but £200 might. And so you may perceive it is a great abatement of a man's countenance to take away

[‡] *Some have gains by the alteration of the coin.*

[§] *Who has loss by the alteration of the coin.*

[36] *Manurance:* the tenure, management, or cultivation of land.

[37] *Manner* (archaic spelling of *manure*): cultivate.

the third part of his living. And therefore, gentlemen do study so much the increase of their lands and the enhancing of their rents and to take farms and pastures into their own hands, as you see they do, and all to seek to maintain their countenance as their predecessors did; and yet they come short of that which makes best shift therein. Some other seeing the charges of household increase so much as by no provision they can make it can be helped, give over their households and get them chambers in London or about the Court and there spend their time; some of them with a servant or two, where he was wont to keep thirty or forty persons daily in his house and to do good in the country in keeping good order and rule among his neighbors. The other sort be yeomen, servingmen, and men of war that having but their old stinted wages cannot find themselves therewith as they might beforetime without rapine or spoil. As you know, 6*d*. a day now will not go so far as 4*d*. would beforetime, and therefore you have men so unwilling to serve the King nowadays from that they were wont to be. Also where 40*s*. a year was good honest man's wages for a yeoman before this time and 20*d*. a week board wages sufficient, now double as much scant will bear their charges.

KNIGHT. That is long of their excess as well in apparel as in fare; for nowadays servingmen go more costly in apparel and look to fare more daintily than their masters were wont to do in times past.

DOCTOR.[II] No doubt that is one great cause of the greater charge of household, for I know when a servingman was content to go in a Kendal coat[38] in summer and in a frieze coat in winter and with a plain white hose made meet for his body and with a piece of beef or some other dish of sodden[39] meat all the week long. Now he will look to have at the least for summer a coat of the finest cloth that may

[II] *Of excess in apparel and fare.*

[38] *Kendal coat:* a coat made of the coarse cloth produced in the Kendal district.

[39] *Sodden:* boiled.

be got for money and his hose of the finest kersey and that
of some strange dye as Flanders dye or some a French
puke [40] that a prince or great lord can wear no finer if he
wear cloth. Then their coats shall be garded,[41] cut, and
stitched, and the breeches of their hose so drawn with silk
that the workmanship shall far pass the price of the stuff.
And this thing is not restrained as it should be, but rather
cherished of their masters; one striving with another who
may be most proud and whose retinue may go most lavish
and gay for a time of show, whereas through such excesses
they are fain all the rest of the year to keep the fewer
servants. And so in excess of meats, they fare at some times
in the year that in the whole year after they keep either no
house at all or if they do it shall be very small. Like excesses,
as well in apparel as in fare, were used in Rome a little
before the decline of the Empire, so as wise men have
thought it was the occasion of the decay thereof. And therefore Cato and divers wise senators at that time would have
had laws made for restraint of such excess and for that,
through the insolence of some that maintained the contrary,
the same were not duly executed, such pride ensued there
and of pride division and through division utter desolation
for the Commonweal. I pray God this realm may beware by
that example, especially London, the head of this empire,
where such excesses, by reason the wealth that is of all this
realm is heaped up as the corn of a field into a barn, be
most used; for in other parts commonly of this realm, the
law of necessity keeps men in good case for exceeding
either in apparel or fare. I think we were as much dreaded
or more of our enemies when our gentlemen went simply
and our servingmen plainly without cut or garde, bearing
their heavy sword and buckler on their thighs instead of
cuts and gardes and light dancing swords; and when they
rode carrying good spears in their hands instead of white

[40] *Puke:* a superior quality of woolen cloth dyed a special blue-
black color.
[41] *Garded* (archaic spelling of *guarded*): trimmed; usually refers
to an ornamental border.

rods which they carry now more like ladies or gentlewomen than men, all which delicacies make our men clean effeminate and without strength.

KNIGHT. We may thank our long peace and quietness within the realm that men be not forced to ride so strong; it was a troubled world, as well within the realm as without, when men went and rode as you speak.

DOCTOR. What can you tell what time or how soon such a world may come again? Wise men do say that in peace men must look and provide for war and in war again for peace.[†] If men might be always sure of peace and there needed [42] no man to keep men at all. But since it is otherwise and that the iniquity of men is such as they cannot be long without war, and that we reckon here in England our chief strength to be in our servingmen and yeomen, it were wisdom to exercise them in time of peace somewhat with such apparel, fare, and hardness as they must needs sustain in time of war. Then the same shall be no novelty to them when they come to it and their bodies shall be stronger and harder to bear that that they were somewhat accustomed withal before. Let this I say be of [no] credit, if delicacy and tenderness was not the most occasion of the subduing of the greatest empires.

KNIGHT. Surely you say very well and that which sounds to good reason. I must needs allow that I have found true myself, for my men are so tenderly used in the time of peace that they cannot away with [43] any heavy armor in time of war but either shirts of mail or coats of linen rags which at a shock may happen deceive us. Then what say you by our buildings that we have here in England of late days, far more excessive than at any time heretofore? Does

[†] *In peace look for war.*

[42] *And there needed:* i.e., there would be no need for any man to keep . . . .

[43] *Away with:* wear, bear, abide.

not that impoverish the realm and cause men to keep less houses?

DOCTOR.‡ I say that all these things be tokens of ornaments of peace, and that, no doubt, is cause of less households since the building and trimming of these houses spends away that that should be otherwise spent in household. But it does not impoverish the realm at all, for all the expense of buildings for the most part is spent among ourselves and among our neighbors and countrymen as among carpenters, masons, and laborers; except men will fall to gilding or painting of these houses for in that much treasure may be spent and to no use. Also the arras, verders,⁴⁴ and tapestry work, wherewith they be hanged, commonly conveys over into Flanders and other strange countries where they be had for much of our treasure.

KNIGHT. Sir, yet I must remember you of one thing more which men do suppose to be a great occasion of the spending of the treasure abroad and that is where there is come to the King's hands of late much treasure by reason of monasteries, colleges, and chantries dissolved, which men suppose has been the cause two manner of ways that there is less treasure abroad in the realm. One is because the revenues of the said places dissolved heretofore were spent in the country and went from hand to hand there for victuals, cloth, and other things and now are gone to one place out of the country. Another is that divers men, which had any riches or wealth, uttered the same to buy parcel of the said dissolved lands, lying commodious for them, whereby one way and other the whole riches of the country is swept away.

DOCTOR. Truth it is also that makes the country abroad bare for the time and had kept it so still if the King's

‡ *Of excess in building.*

⁴⁴ *Verders* (archaic spelling of *verdures*): hangings depicting gardens and woods.

Majesty had not dispersed the same lands abroad among them in the country again. But now that His Highness has parted with a great deal of those possessions, part by gift and part by sale, treasure should shortly increase again abroad as much as ever it was if it be not let by other means. So that I take that to be no great cause of the dearth that we have; for the soil is not taken away, but the possession thereof is only transferred from one kind of person to another.

KNIGHT. Then to return again to the matter of the coin where we left: I have heard your conceit how the alteration thereof does some men no harm, as buyers and sellers; some other it does good unto, as farmers that had land at the old rent; and some other, as gentlemen, men of war, servingmen, and all other living by any rated and stinted rent or stipend, are great losers by it. But I heard you say it was so much withal to the loss of the King's Majesty that it might be to the great peril not only of his royal estate, but also of the whole realm in process of time. I marvel how it should be so for I heard wise men say that the King's Highness father did win inestimable great sums by the alteration of the coin.

DOCTOR.[§] So it was for the time; but I liken that gains to such, as men have when men sell away their lands, to have the greater sum at one time and ever after to lose the continual increase that should grow thereof. For you know all the treasure of this realm must once in few years come to the King's Highness hands, by one means or other, and from him it should go abroad again to his subjects, as all springs run to the ocean sea and out of it are they spread abroad again. Then as they came in of late in good metal, they came forth in such as you now see. And albeit it seems at the first face to impoverish but the subjects only, at length it is to be searched lest it do impoverish the King's Highness; and then if His Grace should want, in time of war specially, suf-

§ *How the alteration of the coin is most loss to the King.*

ficient treasure to pay for armor, weapons, tackling of ships, guns, and other artillery necessary for the war and could by no means have of his subjects wherewith to buy the same, what case should His Grace be in and his realm? Surely in very evil. And therefore these coins and treasure be not without cause called of wise men *nervi bellorum,*|| that is to say, "the sinews of war." And that is the greatest danger that I do consider should grow for want of treasure to the King and his realm; for though the King's Highness may have what coin he will current within his realm, yet the strangers cannot be compelled to take them. And I grant, if men might live within themselves altogether without borrowing of any other thing outward, we might devise what coin we would; but since we must have need of other and they of us, we must frame our things not after our own fantasies but to follow the common market of all the world, and we may not set the price of things at our pleasure but follow the price of the universal market of the world. I grant also that brass has been coined ere this, yea, and leather in some places; but I read that that was at an extreme need, which thing is not to be followed as an example but to be eschewed as long as may be possible. Also I hear say that in France and Flanders there goes abroad such coin at these days but that does not exile all other good coin, but they be current withal and plenty thereof, howsoever they use it. And because I have no experience of their usage there, how both coins are used, therefore I would think it wisdom we did learn of them how we might use the one and the other, keeping either of them at like rate as they do; so that they should never desire any of our coin for any greater value than they be esteemed at with them, nor we theirs for any greater estimate with us than with them. And then should we be sure to keep our treasure at a stay. And as for recovering of old treasure that is already gone,† there might be order that some commodity of ours were so restrained

|| *Money are called* nervi bellorum.
† *For recovery of our treasure home again.*

from them that it should not be sold but for silver or gold
or the third part, or half, in such coin as is universally current. And chiefly our treasure might be soon recovered by
these two means: first, if we forbade the bringing in and
selling of so many trifles, as I before rehearsed, to be brought
us from beyond the seas, and that nothing made beyond the
sea of our commodities should be sold here; and secondly,
if we forbade that none of our commodities should pass unwrought oversea, which, being wrought here and sold over,
should bring in infinite treasure in short time.

KNIGHT.   Marry, and there you be contrary to the opinions
of many a great wise man which think it better that all our
wool were sold over the sea unwrought than any clothiers
should be set at work withal within this realm.

DOCTOR.   That were a strange thing in my opinion that any
man should think so, and what should move them to be of
that opinion I pray you?

KNIGHT.‡   I will tell you. They take it that all these insur-
rections do stir by occasion of these clothiers. For when our
clothiers lack vent oversea, there is a great multitude of these
clothiers idle, and when they be idle, they then assemble in
companies and murmur for lack of living and so pick one
quarrel or other to stir the poor commons, that be as idle
as they, to a commotion. And sometime, by occasion of
wars, there must needs be some stay of cloths so as they
cannot always have sale or vent; at every which time, if the
said clothiers should take occasion of commotion, they think
it were better that there were none of them in the realm
at all and consequently that the wool were uttered unwrought oversea than to have it wrought here.

DOCTOR.   So it may seem to them that consider one inconvenience and not another. Surely, whosoever has many
persons under his governance shall have much ado to govern

‡ *Whether all our wool were expedient to be sold over unwrought.*

them in quiet, and he that has a great family shall have sometimes trouble in the ruling of them. Yet were it but a mean policy either for a prince to diminish his number or for a master of a house to put away his servants because he would not have any trouble with the governance of them. He that would so do might be well resembled to a man that should sell his land because he would not be troubled with the account of it. I think it meeter that we did not only increase the feat of clothing but also invent divers other more feats and occupations whereby our people might be set at work rather than take away any occupation from them, specially such as clothing is that sets so many thousands at work and enriches both town and country where it is occupied. In Venice, as I heard, and in many other places beyond the sea, they reward and cherish every man that brings in any new art or mystery whereby the people might be set to work with such thing as should both find [45] their workmen and also bring some treasure or other commodity into the country.[s] And shall we contrariwise labor to destroy our best and most profitable trade which is by clothing? I would know what thing else might bring us treasure from strange parts or wherewith so many of our people should be set at work as have now their livings by clothing if that occupation were laid down?

KNIGHT. Marry, we might have treasure enough from outward parts for our wools though none were wrought within the realm. And as for an occupation to set our clothiers to work, they might be set to the plow and husbandry, and that should make husbandry to be more occupied and grazing less when all these people that now do occupy clothing shall fall to husbandry.

DOCTOR. As to the first that you said, that wool is sufficient to bring in treasure. If it were, as it is not indeed, yet that

[s] *Mysteries are to be increased rather than diminished.*
[45] *Find:* i.e., find a living for.

feat were not for the Commonweal nor continuance of the realm. For when every man would fall to breed sheep to increase wool and so at length all other occupations should be set aside and breeding of sheep only occupied, then you know that a few sheepmasters would serve for a whole shire; so in process of time, the multitude of the King's subjects would be worn away and none left but a few shepherds which were no number sufficient to serve the King at his need or defend this realm from enemies. As to the other part of your tale whereby you would that these clothiers should fall from that occupation to husbandry; how could so many, added to them that occupy husbandry already, get their livings by the same when they that be husbandmen now have but a scant living thereby? And if you would say to me that they should have free vent and sale of their corn oversea, then comes the same inconvenience that you thought to avoid before by putting them from clothing: for some years it should happen, either for wars or by reason of plenty in all parts beyond the seas, that they should have no vent of their corn and then be driven to be idle; and consequently, for lack of living, to assemble together and make like uproars as you spoke of before. They have in France more handicrafts occupied and a greater multitude of artificers than we have by a great deal, and for all that they have made many great stirs and commotions there before this. Yet they will not destroy artificers for they know that the highest princes of them all without such artificers could not maintain their estate. Do not all their tolls, customs, taxes, tallages, and subsidies chiefly grow by such artificers? What King can maintain his estate with his yearly revenues only growing of his lands? For as many servants in a house well set on work gains every man to their master, so does [every] artificer in a realm gain each somewhat, and altogether a great mass, to the King and his realm every year.

KNIGHT. Well you have heard what mind many wiser men than I am be of.

DOCTOR. I perceive that there be many great men of that
opinion in this realm or else they had not doubled the
custom of cloth nor charged all cloth made within the realm
with 12*d*. in every pound in the last subsidy; which was the
very high way to make clothiers to give up their occupying,
as I fear it has done and bred much of the inconvenience
that you saw here this last summer, and is like to be occasion
of more if they hold on in that opinion. And now, because
we are entered into communication of artificers, I will make
this division of them.^{||} Some of them do but bring money
out of the country; some other that which they get they do
spend again in the country; and the third sort of artificers is
of them that do bring in the treasure into the country. Of
the first sort [†] I reckon all mercers, grocers, vintners, haberdashers, milliners, and such as do sell wares growing beyond
the seas and do fetch out our treasure for the same, which
kind of artificers, as I reckon them, tolerable and yet not
necessary in a Commonweal, but they might be best spared
of all other—yet if we had not other artificers to bring in
as much treasure as they do bring forth, we should be great
losers by them. Of the second sort be these: [‡] shoemakers,
tailors, carpenters, masons, tilers, butchers, brewers, bakers,
and victualers of all sorts which, like as they get their living
in the country, so they spend it, but they bring in no
treasure unto us. Therefore we must cherish well the third
sort [§] and these be clothiers, tanners, cappers, and worsted
makers; only that I know which by their mysteries and faculties do bring in any treasure. As for our wool, fells, tin,
lead, butter, and cheese, these be commodities that the
ground bears, requiring the industry of a few persons, and
if we should only trust to such and devise nothing else to
occupy ourselves with, a few persons would serve for the
rearing of such things and few also it would find. And so
should our realm be but like a grange, better furnished with

---

^{||} *Three sorts of mysteries.*   [†] *One brings out our treasure.*
[‡] *Another spends that they get in the same country again.*
[§] *The third sort brings in treasure and therefore must be cherished.*

beasts than with men; whereby it might be subject to other
nations about, which is the more to be feared and eschewed
because the country of his own kind is more apt to bring
forth such things as be for the breed of cattle than for such
things as be for the nourishment of men—if Pomponius Mela
be to be believed,|| which, describing this island, said thus,
*Plana, ingens, fecunda, verum iis que benignius pecora alunt
quam homines,* that is to say, "It is plain, large, and plentiful
but of those things that nourish beasts more kindly than
men." So many forests, chases, parks, marshes, and waste
grounds, being more here than commonly elsewhere, declare
the same not to be all in vain that he affirms. It has not so
much arable ground, vines, olives, fruits, and such as be both
most necessary for the food of men, and as they require
many hands in the culture so they find most persons food,
as France and divers other countries have. Therefore as
much ground as be here apt for those things would be
turned, as much as may be, to such uses as may find most
persons. And over that, towns and cities would be replen-
ished with all kind of artificers, not only clothiers which is
as it were our natural occupation, but with cappers, glovers,
papermakers, glaziers, pointers,[47] goldsmiths, blacksmiths of
all sorts, coverlet makers, needlemakers, pinners,[48] and such
other; so as we should not only have enough of such things
to serve our realm and save an infinite treasure that goes
now over for many of the same, but also might spare of
such things ready wrought to be sold over, whereby we
should fetch again other necessary commodities or treasures.
And this should both replenish the realm of people able to
defend it and also save and win much treasure to the same.†
Such occupations alone do enrich divers countries that else
be barren of themselves, and what riches they bring to the

|| *Pomponius Mela.*[46]

† *Mysteries do enrich countries that be else barren.*

[46] Pomponius Mela was a Roman geographer who wrote a treatise
entitled *De situ orbis.*

[47] *Pointers:* makers of lace "points" for decorative tags on clothes.

[48] *Pinners:* makers of pins.

countries where they be well used the countries of Flanders and Germany do well declare, where through such occupations it has so many and that so wealthy cities that it were incredible in so little ground to be. Wherefore in my mind they are far wide of right consideration that would have either none or else less clothing within this realm because sometimes it is occasion of busyness and tumults for lack of vent. There is nothing every way so commodious or necessary for men's use but it is sometime by ill handling occasion of some displeasure, no, not fire and water that be so necessary as nothing can be more.

KNIGHT.   Yea, Master Doctor, but we stand not in like case as France or Flanders that you speak of do. If they have not vent one way, they may have it another way always for the firm land is round about them in manner; if they be at war with one neighbor, they will be friends with another to whose countries they may send their commodities to sell.

DOCTOR.‡   So may we be if we be wise, keep one friend or other always in hand. Who will be so mad, being a private man, but he will be sure to do so? Let wise men consider what friends this realm has had in times past, and if they be now lost or intercepted another way since, let us purchase other for them or else give as little occasion of breach with our neighbors as may be. The wise man, as I remember, says in Ecclesiastes *Non bonum homini esse solum.* [49]

KNIGHT.§   Also in France they have divers bands of men of arms in divers places of the realm to repress such tumults quickly if any should arise. If we had the like here, we might be bold to have as many artificers as they have.

‡ *Alliances with strangers are to be purchased and kept.*
§ *Whether gendarmes were necessary here as in France.*
[49] *Non bonum homini esse solum:* "It is not good for man to be alone"; the quotation is from Gen. 2:18, not Ecclesiastes.

HUSBANDMAN. God forbid that ever we had any such tyrants come amongst us; for, as they say, such will, in the country of France, take poor men's hens, chickens, pigs, and other provision and pay nothing for it except it be an ill turn as to ravish his wife or his daughter for it.

MERCHANTMAN. And even likewise said the merchantman, adding thereto that he thought that would rather be occasion of commotions to be stirred than to be quenched; for, as he said, the stomachs of Englishmen would never bear that—to suffer such injury and reproaches as he heard that such used to do to the subjects of France which in reproach they call peasants.

KNIGHT. Marry, the King our master might restrain them well enough for doing outrages upon great pains.

DOCTOR. What and it were scant in his power to do it? The Romans had sometime such men of arms in divers places, for defense of the empire it was thought, which at length overthrew the same. Julius Caesar does that declare; and many times after that, when the Emperors died, the men of war erected what Emperor they listed, sometime of a slave or bondman, contrary to the election of the Senate of Rome, being chief councilors of the empire, till the whole empire was clean destroyed. It is not for commotions of the subjects that France also keeps such but the state and necessity of the country which is environed about with enemies, and neither sea nor wall between them, against whose inroads and invasions they maintain those men of war of necessity. They would fain lay them down, and they dared [50] for fear of their neighbors. And some wise men among them have said and written that the same men of arms may be the destruction of their kingdom at length. And besides that, neither the largeness of our dominion nor situation of the

[50] *And they dared:* i.e., if they dared.

same toward other countries does require such men. Nor
yet the revenues of this realm is able to make up the like
number with France, and then if we should make a less
number, we should declare ourselves inferior in power to
France to whom we have heretofore been counted superior
in success through the stoutness of our subjects only.[II] And
therefore I would not have a small sore cured by a greater
grief, nor for avoiding of sedition popular, which happens
very seldom and soon quenched, to bring in a continual
yoke and charge both to the King and his people.

KNIGHT.   You say well, and so as I can say no more against
your sentence; but yet I would wish your saying could
satisfy other men as well as it does me.

DOCTOR.   Well now, it is time to make an end. I have
troubled you with a long and tedious talk.

KNIGHT.   I would be content to be troubled longer on that
sort.

MERCHANTMAN AND CAPPER.   And so could we, though it
were all this day, but for troubling of yourself, gentle
Master Doctor.

KNIGHT.   Yet the most necessary point which you speak of
is yet behind. That is, how these things may be remedied,
and therefore we go not from you till we may have your
advice herein.

DOCTOR.   A God's name, I will show my fantasy in that
part, but let us first go to supper.
    And so we went together to our supper where our host
had prepared honestly for us.

[II] *A less grief would not be helped with a great sore.*

The Third Dialogue,
wherein are devised the remedies
for the said griefs

K<small>NIGHT.</small> After we had well refreshed ourselves at supper, I thought long till I had known the judgment of Master Doctor about the remedies of the things above remembered, how he thought they might best be redressed, and with least danger or alteration of things, and therefore I said to him thus: Since you have declared unto us, good Master Doctor, our diseases and also the occasions thereof, we pray you leave us not destitute of convenient remedies for the same. You have persuaded us fully, and we perceive it well ourselves, that we are not now in so good state as we have been in times past, and you have shewed us provable occasions that have brought us to that case; therefore, now we pray you show us what might remedy these our griefs.

D<small>OCTOR.</small> When a man does perceive his grief and the occasion also of the same, he is in a good way of amendment; for knowing the occasion of the grief a man may soon avoid the same occasion and that being avoided the grief is also taken; for as the Philosopher says *Sublata causa tollitur effectus.*[1] But let us briefly recount the griefs and then the occasions thereof and thirdly go to the inquisition of the remedies for the same: † first, this general and universal dearth is the chiefest grief that all men complain most on; secondly, the exhausting of the treasure of this realm;

† *The common griefs.*

[1] *Sublata causa tollitur effectus:* "The removal of the principal cause takes away the effect."

thirdly, enclosures and turning of arable ground to pasture; fourthly, decaying of towns, townships, and villages; and last, division and diversity of opinions in religion. The occasions or causes of these, although I have before diversely declared after the diversity of men's minds and opinions, yet here I will take to be the same, but only such as I think verily to be the very just occasions indeed. For as I shewed you before, divers men diversely judge this or that to be the cause or occasion of this or that grief. And because there may be divers causes of one thing and yet but one principal cause that brings forth the thing to pass, let us seek out that cause, omitting all the mean causes which are driven forward by the first original cause ‡—as in a great press going in at a straight the foremost is driven by him that is next him, and the next by him that follows him, and the third by some violent and strong thing that drives him forward, which is the first and principal cause of the putting forward of the rest that is before him; if he were put back and stayed, all they that go before him stay withal. To make this more plain unto you, as in a clock there be many wheels yet the first wheel being stirred it drives the next, and that the third, and so forth until the last that moves the instrument that strikes the clock. So in making of a house there is the master that would have the house made, there is the carpenter, and there is the stuff to make the house withal; the stuff never stirs till the workman do set it forward, the workman never travails but as the master provokes him with good wages, and so he is the principal cause of this housemaking. And this cause is of clerks called "efficient" as that that brings the thing principally to effect. Persuade this man to let this building alone and the house shall never come to pass. Yet the house cannot be made without the stuff and workmen, and therefore they be called *Causa sine quibus non* [2] and some other *Materiales* and *Formales*, but

‡ *The original cause of everything is to be searched.*
[2] *Causa sine quibus non*: essentials; the prime moving cause.

all comes to one purpose.§ It is the efficient cause that is the principal cause, without removing of which cause the thing cannot be remedied. And because it was grafted in every man's judgment that the cause of anything being taken away the effect is taken away withal, therefore men took the causes of these things that we talk of without judgment, not discerning the principal cause from the mean causes; that by taking away these causes that be but secondary, as it were, they were never the nearer to remedy the thing they went about. Much like the wife of Ajax,‖ that lost her husband in the ship called Argos, wished that those fir beams had never been felled in Peleius wood,[3] whereof the said ship was made; when that was not the efficient cause of the losing of her husband, but the wildfire cast in the said ship which did set it on fire. Such causes, as they be, be called "remote," as it were too far off, so they be also idle and of no operation of themselves without some other to set them to work. And perchance I (while I digress so far from my matter) shall be thought to go as far from my purpose; yet to come to our matter and to apply this that I have said to the same. Some think this dearth begins by the tenant in selling his wares so dear, some other by the lord in raising his land so high, and some by those enclosures, and some other by the raising of our coin or alteration of the same. Therefore some, by taking some one of these things away (as their opinion shewed them to be the principal cause of this dearth), thought to remedy this dearth; but, as the trial of the thing shewed, they touched not the cause efficient or principal, and therefore their device took no place.† And if they had, the thing had been remedied forthwith; for it is proper to the principal cause that as soon as it is taken away the effect is removed also. Yet I confess all these things rise together with this dearth that every of them should seem

§ *Divers sorts of causes there be.* ‖ *Cicero in* op.

† Sublata causa tollitur effectus.

[3] *Peleius wood:* from Mount Pelion in Thessaly. The author errs in his allusion for Ajax was not one of the Argonauts.

to be the cause of it. Nevertheless, that is no good proof
that they should be the causes of it, no more than was the
steeple made at Dover the cause of the decay of the haven
at Dover because the haven began to decay the same time
that the steeple began to be built. Nor yet, though some of
these be cause of the other, indeed, yet they be not all the
efficient causes of this dearth. But as I have said before of
men thrusting one another in a throng, one driving another
and but one first of all that was the chief cause of that force,
so in this matter that we talk of there is some one thing that
is the original cause of these causes, that be as it were secondary, and makes them to be the causes of other.[*] As I
take the raising of the prices of all victuals at the husbandman's hand is the cause of the raising of the rent of his
lands; and that gentlemen fall so much to take farms to their
[hands], lest they be driven to buy their provision so dear;
and that is a great cause again that enclosures is the more
used. For gentlemen having much lands in their hands, not
being able to weld all and see it mannered in husbandry
which requires the industry, labor, and governance of a
great many of persons, do convert most part of that land to
pastures wherein is required both less charges of persons
and of the which nevertheless comes more clear gains. Thus
one thing hangs upon another and sets forward one another,
but one first of all is the chief cause of all this circular
motion and impulsion. I shewed awhile ere that I thought
the chief cause was not in the husbandman nor yet in the
gentleman. Let us see whether it be in the merchantman. It
appears so; by reason all wares bought of him are dearer
now, far than they were wont to be, the husbandman is
driven to sell his commodities dearer. Now that the matter
is brought to you, Master Merchant, how can you avoid
the cause from being in you?

MERCHANTMAN. Sir, easily enough; for as we now sell
dearer all things than we were wont, so we buy dearer all

[*] *How one thing is cause of another.*

things of strangers. And therefore let them put the matter from them there; we disburden ourselves of this fault.

DOCTOR. And they be not here to make answer. If they were, I would ask them why they sell their wares dearer now than they were wont to do.

MERCHANTMAN.[8] Marry, and to that I heard many of them answer ere this, when they were asked that question, two manner of ways. One was they sold indeed no dearer than they were wont to do, saying, for proof thereof, that they would take for their commodities as much and no more of our commodities than they were wont to do; as for our tod of wool they would give as much wine, spice, or silk as they were wont to give for so much, yea, for an ounce of our silver or gold as much stuff as ever was given for the same. And their other answer was that if we reckoned that they did sell their wares dearer because they demanded more pieces of our coin for the same than they were wont to do, that was not their fault, they said, but ours that made our pieces less or less worth than they were in times past. Therefore they demanded the more pieces of them for their wares, saying they cared not what names we would give our coins, they would consider the quantity and right value of it that they were esteemed at everywhere through the world.

KNIGHT. Then I would have answered him thereof this sort: If they came hither but for our commodities, what made it the matter to them what value or quantity our coin were of, so they might have as much of our commodities for the same as they were wont to do? If they came again for our silver and gold, it was never lawful nor yet is expedient they should have any from us. Wherefore I would think that was no cause wherefore they should sell their wares dearer than they were wont.

---

[8] *The strangers' answer touching this dearth.*

DOCTOR. Then he might have answered again that it chanced not always together that when they had wares which we wanted we had again all those wares that they looked for. And therefore, they, having perchance more wares necessary for us than we had of such wares as they looked for, would be glad to receive of us such stuff current in most places as might buy that they looked for elsewhere at their pleasure and that, they will say, was not our coin. And as for our laws of not transporting oversea any gold or silver, they passed not thereof, so they might have the same once conveyed them as they had many ways to have it so, which I have before remembered. Finally, he might say that we had not indeed our coin in that estimate ourselves that by the name they pretended, but esteemed both the value and quantity of the stuff it was made of; for if they had brought to us half an ounce of silver we would not take it for an ounce, nor if they brought us brass mingled with silver we would not take it for pure silver. And if we would not so take it at their hands, why should they take it otherwise at ours? Then they saw no man here but would rather have a cup of silver than a cup of brass, no, not the masters of our mints though they would otherwise persuade the one to be as good as the other. Wherefore, seeing us esteem the one indeed better than the other, as all the world does beside, why should they not esteem our coin after the quantity and value of the substance thereof, both after the rate it was esteemed among us and also every other where? And so as in [more] pieces now there is but the value that was in fewer pieces before, therefore they demand greater number of pieces but yet the like value in substance that they were wont to demand for their wares. Now let us see whether now goes the cause of this matter from the stranger. For methinks he has reasonably excused himself and put it from him.

KNIGHT. By your tale it must be in the coin and consequently in the King's Highness by whose commandment the same was altered.

DOCTOR.   Yet, perchance it goes further yet. Yea, to such as were the first counselors of that deed, pretending it should be to His Highness' great and notable commodity, which, if His Grace may now perceive to be but a momentary profit and a continual loss both to His Highness and also his whole realm, may be soon revoked again by His Grace. And as a man that intends to heal another by a medicine that he thinks good, though it prove otherwise, is not much to be blamed, no more is the King's Majesty in no wise, in whose time this was not done, nor His Highness' father, which is not to be supposed to have intended thereby no loss but rather commodity to himself and his subjects, to be herein reprehended albeit the thing succeeded beside the purpose.

KNIGHT.   Then you think plainly that this alteration of the coin is the chief and principal cause of this universal dearth?

DOCTOR.|| Yea, no doubt, and of many of the said griefs that we have talked of by means it being the original of all. And that, beside the reason of the thing, being plain enough of itself, also experience and proof does make more plain; for even with the alteration of the coin began this dearth, and as the coin appeared so rose the price of things withal. And this to be true, the few pieces of old coin yet remaining testifies; for you shall have for any of the same coin as much of any ware, either inward or outward, as much as ever was wont to be had for the same, and so as the measure is made less there goes more sum to make up the tale. And because this rises not together at all men's hands, therefore some have great loss and some other great gains thereby, and that makes such a general grudge for the thing. And thus to conclude, I think this alteration of the coin to be the first original cause; that strangers first sell their wares dearer to us and that makes all farmers and tenants that rear any commodity again to sell the same dearer, the dearth thereof makes the

|| *That the alteration of the coin should be the very cause of this dearth.*

gentlemen to sell their rents and to take farms to their hands for their better provision and consequently to enclose more ground.

KNIGHT.** [4]   Now what remedy for all these things?

DOCTOR.[†]   You see now the means yourself, if this be the efficient cause as I do think it is; and I know no mean to amend anything that is amiss but either by another precedent that is well or by art. And if we take the first way, we may take either our Commonweal when it was well for a precedent or another Commonweal that we see well ordered to whose example we might conform our things. If the other way do like us better to do it by art, we must then seek out the right causes of these effects and by taking away the chief and efficient causes the effects be taken away that proceed, as I have often said.

KNIGHT.   I pray you, tell plainly your advice; what causes be those that you would have taken away, and how these things may be amended.

DOCTOR.   I will, under protestation that, if you like it not, you do tell your fantasies [5] to it and reject it; if you like it or any part thereof, use it at your pleasure. I mean, quoth he,[‡] that all the coin now current should be, after a certain day, not current but as men list to take them after the estimation of the stuff; and the old coin, or new, after like value and quantity and names to be only from thence current; and so the coin thoroughly restored to the old rate, goodness, and value.

[†] *Either by example or by art anything must be amended.*

[‡] *The remedy to be only by restoring the coin to the old rate and names.*

[4] All this section ** to ** p. 116 was omitted from the 1581 edition. It was replaced by the section found in Appendix A, Part II.

[5] *Tell your fantasies:* i.e., make your own speculations.

KNIGHT.   All the treasure in this realm is not able to do that by and by at once except it might be amended by a little and a little, some this year and some the next year.

DOCTOR.   How mean you that?

KNIGHT.   I mean thus, to amend the groat by one halfpenny this year and so the next year, another.

DOCTOR.   God forbid that you should advise the King to do so! For that should be a mean, as it has been already, to put the King to charge, and the matter never a whit the better amended.

KNIGHT.   How so?

DOCTOR.   Marry, I will show you if you mean one way thus. If this coin we now have being current the King would mend his new coin, that he makes from henceforth a portion as a penny or an ob in a piece, you will grant when that coin comes abroad the same shall be in just value better by a penny or ob than the other that we have now.[6]

KNIGHT.   Yea, no doubt.

DOCTOR.   Then shall not the other old coin be as current as it abroad?

KNIGHT.   Yes.

DOCTOR.   Well then, when goldsmiths, merchants, and other skilled persons do perceive that the one groat is better than the other and yet that he shall have as much for the worse groat as for the better, will not he lay up the better groat

[6] I.e., if the King made his new coin from the coin now current, restoring the old amount of pure metal to alloy, the new coin would be that much more valuable.

always and turn it to some other use and put forth the worse, being like current abroad? Yea, no doubt, even as they have done of late with the new gold; for they, perceiving the new coin of gold to be better in estimate than the new coin of silver that was made to countervalue it, picked out all the gold as fast as it came forth out of the mint and laid that aside for other uses, so you have now but little new gold more than the old current.[§] And so both the King's Highness is deceived of his treasure and the thing intended never the more brought to pass, and all is because there is no due proportion kept between the coin while the one is better than the other in his degree. And, as I meant to show you another way, if the King's Highness should call in suddenly all his coin now current and set forth the new coin somewhat better, but yet not all so pure as the old, I take a like deceit should grow by his mintners;[7] for while the metals being confounded together cannot be justly proportioned without resolving again of every one to his own kind, the mintners may do what deceit they list and use that uncertainty for their own lucre.[‖] And if in an ounce or two they should be found faulty, then might they say, "We melted together a great quantity, and that lack of our standard in this portion is supplied in another." And so they can never be well burdened to do their duty but left to their own conscience which I fear me will be large enough. And yet this way were but a patching of the thing, and as much as it is mended of one thing one way it should impair another thing another way.

KNIGHT. Then, what and the King would make the groat less and make it pure and other his coins all?

DOCTOR. All should then come to one matter; for I had as lief have ten pounds of brass as one ounce of silver. And it

---

[§] *All the coin being together current must be of equal value in proportion one toward other.*

[‖] *Confusion of metals gives occasion of deceit.*

[7] *Mintners:* the mint officials.

is not in the power of any prince to make the ounce of silver worth twain, nor yet of gold, nor of other metal. And I had as lief have a halfpenny called a halfpenny as have a halfpenny that should be called a penny. Well a man may change the name of things, but the value he cannot in any wise to endure for any space, except we were in such a country as Utopia was imagined to be that had no traffic with any other outward country. And therefore I would have the just and due proportion kept in this coin not only in quality but also in quantity; for if you should admit alteration either in the one or in the other, you must bring in withal many absurdities.[†] For albeit the prince might strike coins of other quantity and of other names than they were of beforetime—though they were so pure—yet because the accounts of men's livings, rents, stipends, debts, and duties use the names of coins heretofore accustomed as pounds, marks, nobles, reals, and shillings, and all writings made by these names cannot alter any of the same, but you must bring much alteration withal in every man's revenues, debts, and duties; as now it appears well by the alteration of the goodness of the coin it has done, which the King's Highness chiefly, and, next His Grace, the noblemen and gentlemen of this realm may well find at their accounts if they consider the matter well.

KNIGHT. That I feel to be true in myself though I know not the reason why; for albeit I may spend now more than I could sixteen years ago, yet I am not able to keep the like house that I did then.

DOCTOR.[‡] No marvel it should be so. You remember, I trust, that I said today morning unto you that the coin is called of Aristotle the common measure of all things. Then put case that you had no rent in money but paid you [8] in

---

[†] *Not only the substance and quantity but also the names of the pieces of the coin must be after the accustomed manner.*

[‡] *That the coin is the common measure. Aristotles* lib. 5 Eth. cap. 5.

[8] I.e., but you were paid.

such necessaries as you must needs occupy—as in so many bushels of corn and so many yards of cloth, the yard and the bushel being of the measure they be now when you did set forth your lands.[§] If the bushel and the yard should be afterward made less by the one-half, and then if you were paid but of so many bushels of corn and so many yards of cloth as you had before in number but yet after the measure that was after made less, might you then feed so many persons and clothe them as you did before?

KNIGHT.   Not by the one-half for so much is taken away of the stuff that I should do it withal by your reckoning. But is the coin a common measure accounted as you say that may take such diminuition or abridgment as other measures may?

DOCTOR.   It is not my saying only. It is Aristotle's, the sharpest philosopher of wit that ever was, as I said before.

KNIGHT.   Marry, if that be true, the King himself is most loser and then his nobles and gentlemen, which is his chief strength in time of need, and all other that are paid by this measure being of old appointed to a certain number of pounds, marks, or shillings. And I perceive they that pay by this new measure, and yet but after the old number, must needs be great gainers.

DOCTOR.   I perceive now you feel the matter yourself?

KNIGHT.   Yes, no doubt it must be thus. But one thing more I must ask you. How they do then in France and Flanders where they have both brass coin, mixed coin, pure silver, and pure gold current together?

DOCTOR.[‖]   I warrant you by keeping of due proportion of every metal toward another, as of brass toward silver a

---

[§] *It is not enough for a man to be paid in like number but also in like quantity.*

[‖] *It made no matter though some coin were of brass so it kept a due proportion of his estate toward silver and gold.*

hundred to one, of silver toward gold twelve to one. For
this proportion of silver toward gold I think cannot be altered by the authority of any prince. For if it might have
been, it should have been ere this by some one needy prince
or other within two thousand years; for so long it is since
Plato, that other great philosopher, was, which for his excellent wisdom was called Divine Plato.[†] He in his dialogue
called *Hipparchus* shows that the said proportion was in his
time between silver and gold, and the same continues now
still; [‡] for twelve ounces of silver is worth but one ounce of
pure gold at this day. And so, when six angels made an ounce
of gold, twenty groats of pure silver—making two ounces
of silver—countervalued an angel. And so 40*d.* in silver answered the 40*s.* in gold.

KNIGHT.　Still, you would have us return from our old path
whence we strayed; but all the mastery is in the devising of
the means how.

DOCTOR.　Surely it requires some sharp and provident device. But that is nothing so hard—nor the inconvenience
growing thereof, as some percase must needs be, so busy [9]
to be provided for—as these be and are like more and more
to grow by the suffering of the coin to be in case [10] it is
now; and things naturally do revert and with less difficulty
to their old trade than to any rare or insolent [11] usage. And
people must needs be pleased with that they were accustomed unto before and will be contented to bear some pain
to bring it thereto.

KNIGHT.　Well, set the case as you would have it and let me
and my friends here see what inconvenience may grow
thereof.

[†] *Plato in* Hipparcho.
[‡] *What proportion was between silver and gold ii thousand years
ago the same is yet at this day.*
[9] *Busy:* likely to give rise to matters requiring attention.
[10] *Case:* condition, state of being or affairs, situation.
[11] *Insolent:* unusual, unaccustomed.

DOCTOR. You put me now to a great matter and exceeding my simple wit; that would be devised by the great wise heads of the council or of the parliament or of some picked number of learned and wise men chosen of them and put together to consult of this matter a great space. I have percase waded further than my part was, to speak so far and to tell that the thing must once be done.

KNIGHT. What harm is it, though we imagined here a whole Commonweal among ourselves, so it be not set forth as though we would needs have it after our devise? This good percase it may do that hear of you, Master Doctor: I may hear some sensible reason that when I come to the parliament, whereof I am unworthy, I may there declare, which might enter into some men's ears that might do good herein; and therefore go through and tell your devise. It shall go not further for us.

DOCTOR. It is dangerous to meddle in the King's matters and specially if it may have any likelihood to diminish his profit.

KNIGHT. True it is, if a man did speak it in place where it should do harm indeed and to that intent.

DOCTOR. I do not so but all to the best purpose—I take God to record—and to the King's Highness most profit, honor, and safety at length; yet some percase will say that pertains not to me to study for. Yet I am a subject, and I owe him not only obedience but also the obsequy [12] I can, either in deed or in devise, and therefore I will put the case thus. Grant the King should make proclamation that, after Michaelmas next coming, there should be no money current within this realm but only after the old rate and that every man should bring in his new coin to the King's mint and there to have bills; that for every ten shillings of new coin

---

[12] *Obseauy:* the rendering of service.

brought in, the King to give them, between Michaelmas and Christmas next after or such a time, an angel noble either in good gold or in good silver of the old value, viz., ten groats to the ounce of silver and six angels to the ounce of gold. I ask what harm should come thereof?

KNIGHT. Marry, no harm at all if it might be so brought to pass. But where should the King have treasure to do it withal? His Grace has neither so much in his own treasure nor yet percase all his subjects withal as would make coin sufficient for the traffic of the whole realm.

DOCTOR.[s] I deny not but it would be a year, two, or three, ere this realm be full furnished as it was before and the King's Highness shall have some want of treasure for a time to do this withal; but the difficulty is not so great as it seems, and that should be all at the beginning. For first, the King's Majesty should have some treasure tried [13] out of this new coin that should be brought into the mint. Some old coin there is yet left in the realm, which would come in to the King for rent if it were in his just estimate; some plate is also left that men would be glad to bring in to coin if they might have it again in pure silver as they were wont to have. And a provision might be in the mean season made that no wool, cloth, or tin, or such like commodities should be uttered forth of the realm but it should be paid for in good gold or silver after the old rate. And if His Grace did provide that men might have bullion coined better cheap than ever they had it before, or yet as good cheap, men would bring in silver apace to the mint.

KNIGHT. This would require a long time ere so much silver and gold were brought in or coined as would serve for all the realm. How should the people in the meantime use their traffic having not coin enough therefor?

---

[s] *How the treasure might be had to reform the coin.*
[13] *Tried:* refined.

DOCTOR. By change of things partly and partly by such proportion of the corrected coin as went abroad till more were made.

KNIGHT. How should the King and gentlemen be paid for their rents the while?

DOCTOR. The King's Highness might be paid of his rent in his own now current and his gentlemen in commodities growing on their tenants' lands, being esteemed at certain prices in lieu of their rent, for the first half year and by the next half year after there should come over for our wools, fells, tin, and lead, and other commodities as much as would pay the King and all other lords their rent in good silver and gold; for I think this, that every tenant rears yearly of some commodity or other as much as may pay [his lord's rent. And the lords again may spare as much of the commodity which they receive of their tenants as will suffice to pay] the King's Majesty his rent at the least. And if there were nothing else to make this matter withal, yet this only thing would in one whole year bring as much good coin as would serve the necessary traffic of the realm; for there is no tenant can well spend more than he gets nor landlord, more than his yearly revenues. And if one among many do exceed, another will spare as much as that comes to. And if one year do not furnish the realm of sufficient coin, another will, and the third will make us as rich as ever we were. For it is not enough for a prince or a realm to have sufficient for one year and so to live, as they say, from hand to mouth as they do now, but to have some store for sudden events either of wars or of dearth.‖ For if we should have wars as we have had and should need either artillery, munitions, or other aid of strangers, it is not the coin that we have now could provide us that. And so likewise if we should have great scarcity of corn within it [14] we should be driven to fetch it from

‖ *A prince ought to have great treasure or else his subjects against all events.*

[14] *It:* i.e., the realm.

outward parts, it is not our money that would purchase it. Then our commodities were not able in a notable scarcity to countervalue it, since now in plenteous years it does bring in but scant enough of things necessary. Then if both war and dearth should come together, as it has ere this, how should we do? Surely we should be in a very hard case and much in the danger of strangers. On the other side, if there were some store of treasure in the realm, though there should happen both wars and dearth yet we were able to abide them for a year, or two, or three. For I had as lief a thousand men had in a dear year one hundred thousand pounds among them in good coin as a thousand barns full of corn worth a hundred pounds apiece; for the money would fetch as much corn as all these barns would come to. And money is, as it were, a storehouse of any commodity you would have, as I have said in our communication before now, which may longest be kept without corruption and easiest carried to and fro for all exchange and is most universally current if it be gold and silver. Nevertheless, but for the encumbrance in carriage, I had as lief have as much brass, tin, or lead in value as the said money should come unto; for they be as meet to abide the long keeping and are universally received in their value, but they are very cumbersome to carry. As, if a man lacked a commodity that were at London, he himself dwelling in Berwick, were it not a great ease for him if he had wares to exchange for the same which he might carry in his sleeves the value of a hundred pound upon a little nag to London with small costs, rather than if he had ware to that value which would require a cart or two to carry it thither?

KNIGHT. Yes, no doubt, but yet he should be surest this way which you spoke last of from robbing.

DOCTOR. That is true, yea, and surest of all if he had neither of both.

KNIGHT. I have heard divers learned men of your sort ere this exclaim against the first inventors of gold and silver because they were occasion of much murders, felonies, and mischiefs; for it is lucre that drives men to all kind of mischief.

DOCTOR.   I wot well they do; as well against the founders of silver and gold as also of iron and steel because also it is the instruments of much murder and slaughter among men. And so I would wish neither of both to be, so it were universally among all.[†] But as if we should cast away our tools and weapons and not other nations that be about, we should make ourselves naked of all defense and be subject to their spoil; so if we alone should cast away our gold and silver because of the harm that comes, not of them but of the evil using of them, and other countries should retain them still, we should weaken ourselves and strengthen them much. Though it be commendable in some private man for contemplation's sake to set aside as much as he may well use of money, it is not necessary for the Commonweal that all men should do so, no more than for all men to be virgins though privately in some it is very commendable.

KNIGHT.   I have heard that princes ere this have coined leather and made it current in time of need.

DOCTOR.   You may say so well that it was a great need then, and for a small time, and yet I never read that more than one did so, called Frederick, surnamed Aenobarbus,[15] one of the Emperors of Almaigne which lived about the year of Our Lord 1193.[‡] He, once in wars, at a time of great need when his money was done and his soldiers ready to depart from him, struck a coin of leather and fixed a nail of silver

---

[†] *That that is universally esteemed must not be rejected of any Commonweal that must have traffic with other.*

[‡] *Coin once made of leather but that in time of great need and for a small space.*

[15] Frederick Aenobarbus, or Frederick Barbarossa, Emperor of Germany, died in 1190. It was Frederick II, however, born in 1194, who issued the leather coins during the siege of Faenza in 1240.

in a piece with his mark, desiring his soldiers to take them for the time in lieu of good coin, promising after the wars finished he would restore them good current money for the same, as he did indeed. By which means he retained his soldiers together and achieved his enterprise, and took in the leather coin and paid them good for it. And so, princes keeping their credit and promise may do wondrous things among their subjects in time of need; which if they do not should bring them to seek help at strangers' hands to their great losses as experience has declared not long ago.

KNIGHT. But here to return where we left; if the King should pay forth good angels as you speak for every ten shillings of this new coin brought to the mint, His Grace's revenues for one whole year would scant serve thereto.

DOCTOR. It were a year's revenues well bestowed to save ten, and it were an honest purchase with one year's rent or two to purchase the ground forever. If the King's Majesty should pay his subjects a good new angel for the noble now current, His Grace should do but as Frederick did and yet His Grace had lever the use of his subjects' coin as reason and necessity so requiring would; yet more than so, by this ordinance also His Grace should win the third part, when for every ten shillings His Grace pays forth but a noble.

KNIGHT. Then if men should have their coin forged or coined for little or nothing, but for the workmen's labors, the King's Highness which has now great advantage by the coinage should be by your ways a great loser.

DOCTOR. So I doubt not the coiners will bear the King and his council in hand. But I would believe them as well herein that they promised before as well and failed, that is, how they could make of brass, silver and of silver, gold. Which thing how well they have brought to pass I report me unto you, much like a dream that chances contrary; for they have turned the while our silver to brass and our gold to I wot not what. And yet one way, I must confess, they have turned the brass to silver and silver to gold, that is, to them-selves-ward.§ But in the meantime they have exhausted the Prince's coffers and his treasure house which is the realm, as the alchemists were wont to do with private men, promis-ing them to multiply when of truth they did diminish; yet they will bear in hand they do still multiply. And so they do in number but diminish in value twice as much again. For instead of one piece, they give forth two, but so as that was worth three of this sort they put forth. And though they persuade the Prince that the gains of all that come to His Grace, yet the most gains cleave by their own fingers. And why? Because the proportion in these confused metals is so uncertain to be known by the assay as the King's officers cannot evenly charge them to keep a certain standard; and if they did, it were not so much to the King's profit as it bears the face, but most of the clear gains comes to them as it was wont to come to the alchemists and multipliers. And that appears well by such as have the feat in hand or have had; how they waxed so suddenly rich as though they had Gyges' ring as the saying is.[16] And this specially appeared by one honest man which I knew had an office awhile about the mint ‖ and continued there, as I heard say, two years or thereabouts and then fell sick and died. But on his deathbed, as he was a very honest man of a good conscience, perceiv-ing that he had got in the office much more than his fee, be-queathed to the King, as I heard credibly, a thousand marks in satisfaction of his unlawful gains had from the King; † much like as men were wont to give to their parish churches for tithes forgotten. Then if such an honest man could get

§ *How the mintners do multiply.*

‖ *Knight his name was.*

† *A mintner's rare example.*

[16] "The riches of Gyges" was the proverbial saying, although Gyges' ring is connected with the legend. Gyges murdered King Candaules and married his widow to become King of Lydia in the seventh cen-tury B.C. Plato tells the story that Gyges murdered the king by means of a gold ring which Gyges had found and which, when worn on the finger, made him invisible.

this much in such a short time, what may another do that has
no conscience in getting his goods? But to answer your ob-
jection; the King gets not so much by his coinage as he loses
in his yearly revenues, customs, subsidies, fines, and such
other profits when the same coin reverts to His Grace's coffers again.

KNIGHT. Well if you had your device that all men after
Michaelmas next should be bound to pay all duties after the
old coin in pure gold or silver, then I put this case; [*] that
since the raising of this coin a man had taken lands at ten
pounds a year which before the enhancing of the coin was
worth but twenty nobles a year, no more than it should be
now if the coin were reformed to the old rate. How should
he and such other do which be a great multitude in this
whole realm? They were like to be undone if they should
be forced to pay their ten pounds a year after the rate of the
old coin.

DOCTOR. That is well remembered of you. Many should
incur great inconvenience if that case were not provided for.
Albeit it were not so universal a hurt to let a few pay so,
that be in that case, as it was to all landlords generally
through the realm to be paid their old rents after the old
rate of the coin that is now. Nevertheless this would be provided [for], seeing it may easily be done, as thus; all men
that take any lands or possessions to farm since the enhancing of the coin to pay for every ten shillings that he should
pay from Michaelmas forward an angel of the corrected
coin of the value of the old angel. And so neither tenant nor
lord grieved nor bargains altered.

KNIGHT. Then I put you this case. If a man were bound
now to pay a hundred pounds to another man, after Michaelmas next coming he must pay it then in the coin that
should then be current which should be more in value by a

[*] *A case to be provided for if the coin were amended touching
men's rent late enhanced.*

hundred nobles than the hundred pounds was [at the] time of the entry of the said obligation; and then he should be a great loser, which were no reason seeing he meant to pay but after the coin now current. How should such do again?

DOCTOR.   Even like provision would be made as in the other case. That such debtors should pay for every ten shillings he did owe by any bond entered since the enhancing of the coin an angel noble. And so the hundred pounds that he should pay by force of the said obligation to be discharged by payment of a hundred marks in this corrected coin and so neither party grieved.

KNIGHT.   How should men that took lands to farm or entered bond of debt before the enhancing of the coin do?

DOCTOR.   As for such lands as were set out before this enhancing or altering of the coin, and so of debts acknowledged, no man ought to be grieved to pay after the old rate; for it was no otherwise meant at the time of the bargains made. Yet this provision was not taken when the coin was altered first, which made all noblemen and gentlemen to smart. And so percase divers other cases like these may occur upon this alteration or rather restitution of things; for in making of any new ordinance it were hard to make it so perfect as it should hinder no one particular person for that were impossible. It is enough if it be so made, as that politic Senator Tully says, that may be profitable to the most number and do hurt but to the fewest. But such cases would be provided for as they do appear. Thus have I told you my simple opinion how I think this universal dearth may be easiest remedied which is caused by ourselves and not by the sending of God. For when God is disposed to send dearth of anything as of corn, cattle, or other victuals, there is nothing can help it devised by man, but only prayer and amendment of life, for whose punishment he sends the same.** [17]

---

[17] End of passage omitted in the 1581 edition.

KNIGHT.   Now that you have so well touched the occasion of this dearth and amendment of the same so fully as I am well satisfied withal, I pray you show me the remedies of these great enclosures whereof all the realm complains so much and has complained long upon. For you have well persuaded how it is a mean of great desolation of this realm and that is long of the great profit that men have by pasture over that they have by tillage that they turn so much to pasture. Now I would fain hear how it might be remedied again; for I have heard this matter of long time often reasoned upon as well in parliament as in council and yet small remedy found therefore that took effect.

DOCTOR.   If I then, after so many wise heads as were in those parliaments and councils, would take upon me to correct as they say *magnificat* and to find a remedy for this thing which they could never do, I might be reckoned very arrogant.

KNIGHT.   Yet tell your fancy therein for, though you miss of the right mean to reform it, it shall be no more shame for you to do so than was it for so many wise men as you spoke of to miss.

DOCTOR.   You say truth. And since I speak nothing in this part that I would have taken as it were a law or a determined thing but as a certain motion for other wise men to consider and to admit or reject as to their better reason shall seem good, therefore—you have boldened me already with your patience to say thus far—I will not spare to declare my mind in this. But still I must keep my ground that I spoke of, that is, to try out the effectual cause of these enclosures and then by taking away of the cause to redress the thing.[§]

KNIGHT.   I pray you do so; for to me it seems very reasonable that you say and agreeable to that I heard a good physi-

[§] Sublata causa tollitur effectu.

cian tell me once when I was sick of an ague when I asked him why he gave me purgations that made me yet weaker than I was, being weak enough already, saying he had more need to give me things that should make me stronger. Then he answered me that choler was the cause of my sickness and that he gave me those purgations to avoid this humor, which, being the cause of my disease, once taken away, the sickness should be rid from me withal. And therefore I pray you use your accustomed order in this matter and tell the cause of these enclosures.

DOCTOR. I showed you before in our communication in the garden the things that I thought to be the cause thereof and partly the remedy of the same.

KNIGHT. So did other men among us tell their fantasies as then, but now we pray you tell us of all those causes you take for the necessary and efficient cause of this matter.

DOCTOR.|| To tell you plainly, it is avarice that I take for the principal cause thereof. But can we devise that all covetousness may be taken from men? No, no more than we can make men to be without ire, without gladness, without fear, and without all affections. What then? We must take away from men the occasion of their covetousness in this part. What is that? The exceeding lucre that they see grow by these enclosures more than by husbandry. And that may be done by any of these two means that I will tell you, either by diminishing the lucre that men have by grazing or else by advancing of the profit of husbandry till it be as good and as profitable to the occupiers as grazing is. For every man, as Plato says, is naturally covetous of lucre † and that wherein they see most lucre they will most gladly exercise. I shewed you before that there is more lucre by grazing of ten acres to the occupier alone than is in the tillage of twenty, and the causes thereof be many. One is that grazing

|| *How enclosures may be remedied.*
† Omnes sunt lucri cupidi.

requires small charge and small labor which in tillage consumes much of the master's gains, though it be true that the tillage of ten acres brings more gains generally among the master and his meinie than the grazing of twenty acres. Another great cause is that whatsoever thing is reared upon grazing has free vent both on this side and also beyond the sea to be sold at the highest penny. It is contrary of all things reared by tillage; for it requires both great charge of servants and of labor, and also if any good cheap be of corn it pays scant for the charge of the tillage, and then if the market do rise, either within the realm or without, the poor husbandman shall be so restrained from selling his corn that he never after shall have any joy to set his plow in the ground, which makes every man forsake tillage and fall to grazing which brings all these enclosures.

KNIGHT.   Now what remedy for that?

DOCTOR.   Marry, as for the first point, that is, touching the unequal charges of tillage and grazing; that cannot be helped in all points by reason the nature of both requires the contrary. Therefore the Latin tongue calls the one that is pasture, *Pratum;* it is as much to say as *Paratum,* "ready." [‡] But the other thing might be remedied; that the husbandman might have as much liberty at all times to sell his corn either within the realm or without as the grazier has to sell his, which would make the husbandmen more willing to occupy their plow. And the one, seeing the other thrive, would turn their pasture to tillage. And though it enhances the market for a time, yet would it cause much more tillage to be used and consequently more corn, which in time of plenty within the realm might bring in much treasure and in time of scarcity would suffice for the realm as I showed you before. And thus with lucre they be enticed to occupy the plow, yea, and with other privileges. I have read in this realm sometime there was such a law as a man that had tres-

[‡] Pratum quasi paratum.

passed the law, of misadventure, might have taken the plow-
tail for his sanctuary. Also the occupation was had so honorable among the Romans that one was taken from holding
the plow to be consul in Rome, who, after his year ended,
thought no scorn to resort to the same feat again. What occupation is so necessary or so profitable for man's life as this
is? Or what mystery is so void of all craft as the same is?
And how little is it regarded? Yea, how much it is vilified
that this late nobility reputes them but as villeins, peasants,
or slaves by whom the proudest of them have their livings.
So that I marvel much there is any, seeing such a vility [18]
and contempt, will occupy the feat of husbandry at all; for
as honor nourishes all sciences,[§] so dishonor must needs decay them. And therefore, if you will have husbandry increased, you must honor and cherish it; that is, to let them
have honest gains thereby. And since that gain shall come
into your country why should you be offended therewith?
Another way is to abate the commodity of grazing; as when
any tax is requisite to be granted to the King's Highness, if
lands be chargeable thereto, to charge one acre of pasture
as much as two acres of arable land or else to burden wools
and fells, and such like things as are reared by grazing, that
pass to the parts beyond the seas unwrought with double
tallage over any corn transported. And so by enhancing of
the profit of tillage and debasing of the profit of grazing, I
doubt not but husbandry would be more occupied and grazing much less, and thereby those enclosures to be broken up.
Also there is one thing of old time ordained in this realm
which being kept unaltered would help hereunto also; that
is, where men are inter-commoners in the common fields and
also have their portions so intermingled one with another,
that, though they would, they could not enclose any part of
the said fields so long as it is so. But of late, divers men, finding greater profit by grazing than by husbandry, have found
the means either to buy their neighbor's parts roundabout

[§] Honos alit artes.
[18] *Vility:* vileness of character or lowliness of condition.

them or else to exchange with them so many acres in this place for so many acres in another whereby they might bring all their lands together and so enclose it. For the avoiding whereof I think verily that it was so of old time ordained that every tenant had his lands not all in one gobbet of every field but interlaced with his neighbor's lands. So as here should be three acres, and then his neighbor should have as many, and over that he other three or four, and so after; the like rate be the most part of the copyholds that I do know in this country, which I think good still were so continued for avoiding of the said enclosures and thus far as to that matter.

MERCHANTMAN.[||] Now that you have well declared your opinion in these matters of the common dearth and enclosures, I pray you tell us your mind what should be the occasion of this decay of the good towns of this realm and of all bridges, highways, and hospitals and how the same may be remedied and relieved again? For these husbandmen and dwellers of the country find not so great lack in the fields abroad, but citizens and burgesses find as much within their walls.

DOCTOR. Since I have begun to take upon me to tell my fantasies in all these things, I will go through. In my opinion, your good occupations heretofore used in the said towns was occasion of their wealth in times past, and the laying down of those occupations again is the cause of the decay of the same towns. Wherefore, if such occupations may be revived again in the same, they would recover their former wealth anon.

MERCHANTMAN. I believe that well that the decay of the occupations was the decay of those towns. But what I pray you was the occasion of such decay of occupations?

DOCTOR.[†] I will tell you. While men were contented with such as were made in the market towns next unto them, then

[||] *Of towns decayed.*
[†] *The occasion of the decay of our towns.*

were they of our towns and cities well set to work; as I
know the time when men were contented with caps, hats,
girdles, and points, and all manner of garments made in the
towns next adjoining, whereby the towns then were well
occupied and set to work and yet the money paid for the
same stuff remained in the country. Now the poorest young
man in the country cannot be contented with a leather girdle or leather points, gloves, knives, or daggers made near
home. And specially, no gentleman can be content to have
either cap, coat, doublet, hose, or shirt made in his country,
but they must have this gear come from London, and yet
many things thereof are not there made but beyond the sea;
whereby the artificers of our good towns are idle and the
occupations in London, and specially of the towns beyond
the sea, are set to work even upon our costs. Therefore I
would wish some stay were devised for coming of so many
trifles from beyond the seas and specially of such things as
might be made here among ourselves or else might be either
all spared or less used among us as these drinking and looking
glasses, painted clothes, perfumed gloves, daggers, knives,
pins, points, aglets, buttons, and a thousand other things of
like sort; as for silks, wines, and spices if there came less over
it made no matter. But specially I would that nothing made
of our commodities as wools, fells, and tin should be brought
from beyond the sea to be sold here but that all these should
be wrought within this realm. Were it not better for us that
our own people should be set to work with such things than
strangers? I am sure twenty thousand persons might be set
to work within this realm, and are set to work beyond the
sea, with those things that now be made beyond the sea and
might be made here. Might not the King's Highness be glad
of any aid whereby he might find a thousand persons
through the whole year and burden his treasure with never
a penny thereof? I think these things might be wrought here
not only sufficient to set so many to work and serve the
realm but also to serve other parts as all kind of cloth, kerseys, worsted, and coverlets [and carpets] of tapestry, caps,
knit sleeves, hose, and petticoats, hats, then paper both white

and brown, parchments, vellum, and all kind of leather ware
as gloves, points, girdles, skins for jerkins, and of our tin all
manner of vessels, and also all kinds of vessels,[19] earthen pots,
tennis balls, tables, cards, chests—since we will needs have
such kind of things—and daggers, knives, hammers, saws,
chisels, axes, and such things made of iron. Might we not be
ashamed to take all these things at strangers' hands and set
such a multitude of their people to work, as I spoke of now,
whose finding and wages we do bear, where all this profit
might be saved within the realm, where it should not go
from us but return to us again from whence it came? And
in setting up of these occupations, I would have them most
preferred and cherished that bring most commodity and
treasure into the country. As you must consider three sorts
of occupations: ‡ one that brings out the treasure; the second
sort that as it brings none forth out of the country so it
brings none in, but that it gets it spends in the country; the
third brings in treasure into the country. Of the first sort
are vintners, milliners, haberdashers, these galleymen, mercers, fustian sellers, grocers, apothecaries that sell us any ware
made beyond the sea, for they do but exhaust the treasure
of the realm. Of the second sort are victualers, innholders,
butchers, bakers, brewers, tailors, card winders, saddlers, carpenters, joiners, masons, blacksmiths, turners, coopers;
which like as they convey no money out of the country so
they bring none in, but where as they get it there they
spend it. Of the third sort be these: clothiers, cappers, worsted makers, pewterers, tanners; which be all that we have
of any art which I can now reckon that brings into the realm
any treasure. Therefore these arts are to be cherished where
they be used, and where they be not they would be set up
and also sciences more; § as making of glasses, making of
swords, daggers, knives, and all tools of iron and steel, also

‡ Mechanic artes trifariam divisae.

§ *That art is to be most cherished in a town that brings most to the
town.*

[19] All the MSS have "glasses" here. The Yelverton scribe probably
made an error, recopying "vessels" from the line above.

making of pins, points, laces, thread, and all manner of paper and parchments. I have heard say that the chief trade of Coventry was heretofore in making of blue thread and then the town was rich even upon that trade in manner only; and now our thread comes all from beyond the seas, wherefore that trade of Coventry is decayed and thereby the town likewise.[II] So Bristol had a great trade by making of points and was the chief mystery [20] that was exercised in the town. And albeit these be but two of the lightest faculties [21] that are, yet were these two great towns chiefly maintained by them. Then consider how many cities might be maintained by the other faculties above rehearsed. I have heard say in Venice, that most flourishing city at these days of all Europe, if they may hear of any cunning craftsman in any faculty, they will find the means to allure him to dwell in their city; for it is a wonder to see what deal of money one good occupier does bring into a town though he himself do not gain to his own commodity but a poor living. As, for example, what money one worsted maker brings into the town where he dwells, and how many have their livings under him, and what wealth he brings to the town where he dwells Norwich may sufficiently declare, which by a few worsted makers that it has is grown to great wealth and riches. So of clothing and capping; but where other cities do allure unto them good workmen, ours will expel them out. As I have known, good workmen, as well smiths and weavers, have come from strange parts to some cities within this realm intending to set up their crafts and, because they were not free there, but specially because they were better workmen than was any in the town, they could not be suffered to work there. Such incorporations had those mysteries in those towns that none might work there in their faculty except they did compound with them first.

[II] *Towns are decayed by some one trade.*
[20] *Mystery:* craft, trade, art.
[21] *Faculties:* arts or trades.

CAPPER. And do you think it is reasonable that a stranger should be as free in a city or town as they that were apprentices there? Then no man would be apprenticed to any occupation if it were so.

DOCTOR. I say not that they shall commonly have like liberty or franchise. But as one craft makes but one particular company of a town or city, so I would have the wealth of the whole city regarded rather than the commodity or franchise of one craft or mystery. For though commonly there should none be admitted there to work but such as is free, yet when a singular good workman in any mystery comes, which by his good knowledge might both instruct them of the town, being of the same faculty, and also bring into the town much commodity beside, I would in that case have private liberties and privileges give place to a public weal and such a man gladly admitted for his excellency to the freedom of the same town without burdening of him with any charge for his first entry or setting up. Yea, where a town is decayed and lacks artificers to furnish the towns with such crafts as other were sometimes well exercised there, or might be by reason of the situation and commodity of the same town, I would have such craftsmen lured out of other places where they be plenty to come to those towns decayed to dwell; offering them their freedom, yea, their house rent free or some stock lent them of the common stock of such towns. And when the town is well furnished of such artificers, then to stay the coming in of foreigners, but while the town lacks inhabitants of artificers it were no policy of the restoration of the town to keep off any strange artificers. For the most part of all towns are maintained by craftsmen of all sorts but specially by those that make any wares to sell out of the country and bring therefore treasure into the same; as clothiers, cappers, worsted makers, hatmakers, pointmakers, pewterers, founders, smiths of all sorts, cutlers, glovers, tanners, parchment-makers, girdlers, purse makers, makers of papers, threadmakers, turners, basket-

makers, and many other such. As for the mercers and haberdashers, vintners and grocers, I cannot see what they do to
a town but find a living to five or six households and instead
thereof impoverish ten times as many. But since men will
needs have silks, wine, and spice, it is as good that men do
spend their money upon such in their own towns as to be
driven to seek the same further. As for the rest of artificers,
as I have said before, even as they take no money out of the
country so they bring none in; as tailors, shoemakers, carpenters, joiners, tilers, masons, butchers, victualers, and such
like. Also another thing I reckon would help much to relieve
our towns decayed, if they would take order that all the
wares made there should have a special mark and that mark
to be set to none but to such as be truly wrought. And also
that every artificer dwelling out of all towns, such as cannot
for the commodity of their occupations be brought to any
town to inhabit as fullers, tanners, clothiers, should be limited to be under the correction of one good town or other;
and they to sell no wares but such as are first approved and
sealed by the town that they are limited unto. And by these
three means—that is to say, first, by staying of wares
wrought beyond the sea which might be wrought within
us from coming in to be sold; secondly, by staying of our
woolens, tin, and fells, and other commodities from passing
over unwrought; and thirdly, by bringing in under the correction of good towns all artificers dwelling in the country making wares to be sold outward and these wares to be
viewed and sealed by the town seal before they should be
sold—I would think our towns might be soon restored to
their ancient wealth or better.

KNIGHT. Now, we pray you, go to the last matter you
spoke of: How this diversity of opinions may be taken away
which troubles the people very sore and makes great sedition and division among them and in manner makes debate
between neighbor and neighbor, father and the son, man
and his wife, which is more to be feared yet than all other
the foresaid losses of worldly goods; for if we were never

so poor and did nevertheless agree among ourselves, we should lick ourselves whole again in short space.

DOCTOR. You say truth. With concord, weak things do increase and wax big, and contrary, with discord, strong things wax weak; [†] and it must needs be true, that [truth] itself Christ says, "Every kingdom divided in itself shall be desolate." Wherefore I cannot forbear to show you my poor opinion how so great a mischief as this is may be avoided out of this Commonweal. And still I will use one trade,[22] as in seeking out the original causes, and by taking away of that to show the remedy. I take the chief cause hereof as well the sins of us that be the ministers of Christ's Holy Word and mysteries as of you that be the flock. And first of ourselves that have swerved altogether from our due course, order, and profession to all kind of carnality not only to the baseness of laymen but far inferior unto them in pride, covetousness, and fleshly lusts. Wherefore you laymen, seeing in us no excellency in our manners indeed, think us unworthy to be your leaders and pastors, or to whose doctrine you should give credit whom you see in living far discrepant from the same.[‡] And therefore you take upon you the judgment of spiritual things, to whom it does not appertain, as one inconvenience draws ever another after him. For so long as we ministers of the church were of those manners and conversation agreeable with our doctrine, so long all men, yea, the great princes of the world and the wisest men, are content to believe our doctrine and to obey us in things concerning the soul. And since we fell from the perfection of life, we grew out of credence and the holy doctrine of Christ suffered slander by our sinful living. So we have given the first occasion of this evil, and you have taken it as an instrument to work this schism withal. And though both do evil therein, yet the remedy ought to begin at the root of this mischief which I take to be in us, the

[†] Concordia paruae res crescunt discordia maximae dilabantur.
[‡] *The occasion of the schism in matters of religion.*
[22] *Use one trade:* i.e., follow one course.

ministers and pastors spiritual. And to be plain with you
and no more to dissemble our own faults than I have done
yours, except we reform ourselves first I can have no great
trust to see this general schism and division in religion utterly taken away. It may perchance with authority be for
a time appeased, but never so as it spring not up again except we reform ourselves first.

KNIGHT.   Marry, I think you have been meetly well dis-
ciplined and corrected already, so as you had good cause to
be reformed, as by taking much of your possessions from
you and in burdening of your benefices with subsidies as
well annual as perpetual and other ways. What other reformation would you have more?

DOCTOR.   Yes, no doubt we have had beating enough if that
would have served, but some masters with little beating
will teach their scholars better than other with more stripes
can do. And again, some scholars will be reformed with less
beating than other. So you and we do now, you in beating
enough but little teaching and we again little regarding your
stripes do learn as little. For notwithstanding those punish-
ments that we have had, the reproaches and revilings and
opening of our faults, see how many of us have reformed
ourselves, yea, so much as in our outward duties whereunto
we are bound both by God's law and our canons, laws, and
decrees. How many more of us have resorted to our benefices to be resident thereon, which not only by the said laws
but also upon great penalties we are bound unto by the laws
of this realm? How many less now than before have studied
to heap benefice upon benefice when we are scant able to
discharge one of them? What better trial or examination is
there now in the admitting of the priests and other ministers
of the church? What more exact search is made by our bishops for worthy men to be admitted to the cure of souls?
What better execution of our canons and decrees do our
bishops, deans, and archdeacons in their visitations now
than they did before? Yea, what better hospitality, residence,

or ministrations, either of the Word or of their other duties, do our prelates and bishops now than they did before? Do they not lurk in their mansions and manor places far from their cathedral churches as they were wont, and scant once in a year will see their principal church where they ought to be continually resident? Be they not as unmeet for preaching the Word of God as ever they were, for all these plagues that God sends to them? But they are so blind they cannot see wherefore they be thus punished and construe it to be for other causes—as by the covetousness of laymen in desiring their possessions, or by hatred conceived against them for not obtaining their purpose at men of the church's hand, or for hatred of the Bishop of Rome, or for that they cannot abide the correction of the church, or such other causes as they imagine with themselves—and think that the indignation against them shortly will slack of itself. But I pray God it does not rather increase as I fear me it will except we amend us the rather. How can men be content to pay the tenth of their goods which they get with their sore labor and sweat of their brows when they cannot have for it again neither ghostly comfort nor bodily? What layman will be anything scrupulous to keep those tithes in his own hands when he sees us do nothing more than he for it? What credence will any man give to our doctrine whom they see so light in living? What reverence will they give our persons in whose manners they see no gravity? Hitherto ** [23] I have spoken but of the abuse of our livings that was due to us by laws; now let us touch somewhat the lucre we devised to ourselves besides all laws, which while we invented too much undue to us we lost much of that which was due to us. Was there any sacrament so holy or so freely instituted of God but we devised a way to get some lucre by the same? Yet Christ bade us give freely that received freely. As of the blessed sacrament of the body and blood of Christ, have we not made a sale of the ministration thereof

---

[23] This section from ** to ** p. 131 was deleted entirely from the 1581 edition.

and sold Masses, some by tale [24] and some in gross as tren-
tals,[25] which thing has brought this holy mystery in a wonderful contempt through our abusing of the same? Is there
any matrimony knit but some fees must come to us therefore? No, not christening but there is somewhat devised to
grow to us thereby? Confession was also by a mean a great
instrument to bring in profit to us when in penance we en-
joined men to give somewhat ever to our churches either
for this thing or for that. Also I do think there is no decree
of orders given but some fees therefore must come to our
chancellors and their clerks. Then how dirges and prayers
were sold it is not to be dissembled, but that he that gave
most money therefore had most said thereof. Yet if prayers
had ensued the alms as voluntary and unprescribed, I think
the same had not done amiss, but limited as a day hire I
think they could not be so valuable; for that they proceeded
not of devotion but for the lucre, and were not esteemed
after the worthiness of the doing thereof so much as by
the number and quantity of the same. But that I refer to be
esteemed of the divines. I discommend nothing but the sale
of these holy things which I can in no wise allow, no, not
so much as a semblance thereof that might bring the people
in any suspect of the same. And therefore the gathering that
is at God's board at Easter, albeit it be for the four offering
days of bread and wine, I would wish that collection to be
forborne at that time, although the parsons, vicars, or proc-
tors should lose some profit thereby. Better it is a small loss
of money than of one soul that might be offended therewith,
which would perhaps think that he could not receive the
communion except he paid for it. We hear what those poor
folk do say when they beg for money to bring them home
from God's table. Those among other things of greater
weight were complained of ere this for reformation and yet
nothing amended, by reason whereof ensued great incon-
veniences, and we pass over all these matters with deaf ears

[24] *By tale:* individually, in this case payment for one Mass.
[25] *Trental:* a series of thirty Masses for the dead.

as though they touched us nothing. And if we do not reform all these things that be notorious to all and manifest
contrary to our laws and canons as for residence, singularity
of benefices, the right and free administration of sacraments,
how can there be any hope that we will reform these things
that are secret between God and us? ** As of our conversation and manners, there be most godly ordinances made by
our laws, by authority of councils general: that all archdeacons should visit in person yearly their precincts; the
bishop, every third year those dioceses to see what is to be
reformed, either privately or generally, that private faults
might be reformed forthwith and the general at the next
synod. And therefore they have their procurations; visit
they do not in person as they ought to do, but by deputies
more for their procuration than for any reformation. The
money is surely gathered but the cause wherefore it was
given nothing kept. The stipend is exacted and the work,
wherefore it was due, undone. Then is there another good
ordinance, and a godly, observed after the like sort where
every bishop should yearly keep a synod in his diocese of
all ecclesiastical persons and every archbishop a synod for
his whole province every third year; [§] that if anything occurred in the diocese worthy reformation, it might be referred to the provincial congregation if it were either doubtful to the bishops or could not be reformed without greater
authority than the bishop's alone. Where be these synods
now kept? Yet they receive every year their synodals of
the poor priests. Of such good ordinances, and godly, there
is nothing kept but that which is our own private commodity which be the procurations and synodals. The other
part wherefore that charge was laid is remitted, the burden
remains and the duty is taken away. Yet better it were that
both the one and the other were taken away than to have
the good part taken and the worst to remain. If they would
say that there needs nowadays no such visitations or synods,
then there never needed none of them; for more things to

[§] Vide Canonem.

be reformed among us were never than now be, nor reformation never more necessary. But our prelates would say they dare make no laws in such synods for fear of praemunire.[26] What need any more laws made than they have already? What should let them to put these in execution that be already, since they have the aid of the temporal laws thereto? ‖ Is there not statutes made in parliaments for residence and for restraining of plurality of benefices which had never need to have been made if we would have put our laws into execution? Are not we worthy to have other men correct us and reform us when we cannot reform ourselves? Is it marvel that we be not of credence when our life and conversation is contrary to our own laws and profession and that the religion of Christ suffers slander through our naughty behavior? Let us be assured therefore that the blood of them that suffers slander or offense in the religion through our defaults shall be once required at our hands. Therefore, if we will have this schism taken away from Christ's church, let us first reform ourselves and put our laws in execution in resorting to our benefices to keep residence and in contenting ourselves with one benefice apiece and with the living that is appointed to us for our ministration without devising of other extraordinary and unlawful gains. For what is more agreeable with reason than a man to spend his time where he has his living? And to do his office for that he has the benefit of? † And seeing every benefice is a man's living, and if it be not, it might be amended until it be a competent living, and everyone requires one whole man's charge what reason is it that one man should have two men's livings and two men's charge, where he

‖ *Look Dr. Collet's sermon.*[27]

† Propter officium datur beneficium.

[26] *Praemunire:* by issuing the royal writ of praemunire which became part of English law in the fourteenth century, the crown could reserve matters for the King's jurisdiction alone and so protect itself from any activities which it considered were a usurpation of its authority by the church.

[27] Dr. John Colet, famous humanist, teacher, and preacher.

is able to discharge but one? Then to have more and discharge the cure of never a one is too far against reason. But
some percase will say there be some of us worthy of greater
preferment than other and one benefice were too little for
such a one. Is there not as many degrees in the variety of
benefices as there is in men's qualities? Yes, forsooth. There
is yet in this realm, thanks be to God, benefices from four
or five thousand marks to twenty marks a year, of sundry
values to endow every man with after his quality and degrees. And if a mean benefice happen to fall, let every man
be content therewith till a better falls. And if he be thought
worthy of a better, let him leave the first and take the better; for the meanest benefice is a sufficient living for some
man which should be destitute of a living if that benefice,
and other like, should be heaped up together in great men's
hands. Yea, I do know that men that have such mean benefices be more commonly resident and keep better hospitality
on the same than they that have greater benefices. It is a
common proverb "It is merry in hall when beards wag all."
Now look through whole dioceses, you shall not find two
persons resident that may dispend forty pound apiece, nor
all of the benefices in a diocese, the fourth person resident
on the same. What temporal office is so far abused as these
be that be spiritual and of greater charge? I pray God send
our prelates eyes to see those enormities, for it should seem
that they are so blinded that they cannot see them. And then
I doubt not but, all delays set apart, they will reform them,
and if they do not, I pray God send our magistrates temporal the mind to reform these things with their secular
power and to study for the reformation of them rather than
for their possessions. Christian princes bear not their sword
in vain, nor is it so strange a thing to see Christian princes
reform the prelates that swerve from their duties. Thus far
be it spoken touching the reformation of us that be ministers of the church. Now to speak of that which is to be
reformed of your part, which be of the laity. You must
understand that all that give themselves to the knowledge
of any faculty are commonly subject to either of two vices,

as the great clerk Tully does report.‡ The one is to take
those things that we know not for things known, as though
we knew them; for the avoiding of which fault men ought
to take both good space and great diligence in consideration
of things ere they come to give judgment of the same. The
other vice is to bestow too great a study and labor about
obscure and hard things and nothing necessary. Let us now
consider and those faults be not among you at these days.§
You be all now studious to know the understanding of Holy
Scriptures, and well; for there can be no better desire, more
honest nor more necessary, for any Christian man. But yet
do you not see many young men, before they have taken
either long time or any good diligence in the consideration
or study of Scripture, take upon them to judge of high matters, being in controversy, giving too quick assent either to
their own invention or to other men's before they have considered what might be said to the contrary? And this fault
is not only seen in men studious of the knowledge of Scripture but also in young students of all other sciences. Shall
you not find a student in the law of the realm, after he has
been at the study of the law not past three years, more
ready to assoil you a doubtful case of the law than either
he himself or any other after he has studied the law twelve
or fourteen years? Yea, no doubt. So it is in a young gram-
marian, logician, rhetorician, and so of all other sciences.
Therefore Pythagoras forbade his scholars to speak the first
five years that they came to him, which lesson I would to
God you would be content to observe before you gave
any judgment in matters of Holy Scripture; and then I doubt
not but after seven years' reading you would, by collation
of one place with another of Scripture, find a greater difficulty therein than you do now and be more scrupulous to
give an answer in high things than you be now. And this
harm comes of rash judgment in that part that when a man
has once uttered his opinion in anything he will think it a

‡ *Cicero* de Offic. lib. 1.
§ *The faults on the part of the laity.*

great shame for him to be brought from that he once has affirmed for truth. Therefore, whatsoever he reads after, he construes it for the maintenance of his opinion, yea, and will force that side not only with his words and persuasions, but also with that power and authority that he has, and will labor to bring others to the same opinion, as many as he can, as though his opinion should be the more true the more fautors [28] that he may get. Many get of the same by such means. If we seek but for the truth, that is not to be judged to be always on that side that gets the overhand by power, authority, or suffrage extorted. It is not like in the disceptation [29] and inquisition of the truth as it is in a fight or a wrestling; for he that has the overhand in those things has the victory and in the other he that is sometimes put to silence or otherwise vanquished in the sight of the world has the victory and conquest of truth on his side. Since we contend but for the knowledge of the truth, what should we divide ourselves into faction and parties? But let the matter be quietly discussed, tried, and examined by men to whom the judgment of such things appertain; [||] and provide in the meantime that neither party do use any violence against the other to bring them by force to this or that side until the whole or most part of them, to whom the discussion of such things appertain unto, freely consent and determine the matter. This is the one way to decide such controversies. And since this contention must once have an end, it were better to take an end betimes than late, when percase more harm shall have ensued of this dangerous schism as has already done in other parts even before our eyes. And in like, things have before this time been seen of such sort as it is too lamentable to be remembered. What loss of Christian men, diminution of the Christian faith, what continual wars has the faction of the Arians been the occasion of? Did it not divide and sever at length all Asia and Africa from the Christian faith? Is not the religion, or rather the

---

[||] *As Constantine the Great did in Arius' time.*

[28] *Fautors:* adherents, partisans.

[29] *Disceptation:* disputation, discussion.

wicked superstition, of the Turk grafted on this Arian's sect?
Did it not take his foundation thereof? As there is no division more dangerous than that which grows of matters of
religion, so it were most expedient and necessary to be
quickly remedied which cannot be done by any other way
than by a synod, general convocation, or council that has
been always, from the time of the apostles who first took
that remedy even to these days, the only way to quiet and
appease all controversies in religion. And no doubt the Holy
Ghost, as his promise is, will be present in every such assembly that is gathered together by one force or labor of
any faction. But now you will say, though we would, for
our part, set aside and be indifferent and use no coercion to
get numbers and voices that should favor our parts, who can
promise that the Bishop of Rome and other prelates will do
the same? Surely, if you did say so, you said a great matter;
for they be men and as much subject to affections as you be.
But I shall be bold after my manner to tell my mind herein
as well as in other things.[†] I take all these matters that be
nowadays in controversy to be of one or other of these
three sorts. That is, either touching religion only, or else
the profits and emoluments of the prelates and ministers of
the church only, or touching partly the one and partly the
other. As touching those articles that concern religion only,
I would wish that they had only the discussion thereof
which ought and have always used to have the judgment of
the same. And as touching the articles that concern the profit
only of ecclesiastical persons, I would have those left to the
discussion of the secular powers, because it concerns secular
things only, where no man needs mistrust but that the magistrates will provide an honorable living for that kind of
man that serve so honorable a room as the ministration of
God's Holy Word and His sacraments. As to the third sort
of things as they be mixed of secular and spiritual things, so
I would wish men of both degrees to consult together for
the division of them. And to be plain I would wish in things

[†] *How this schism might be remedied.*

touching the reformation of the Bishop of Rome, his faculties, he were set apart and some other indifferent persons chosen by Christian princes to direct or be president in the council while his matter is in handling; for no man is meet to be a judge in his own cause. Here I have but briefly touched the sum of things after my simple fantasy referring the allowing or rejecting of all or some of them to your better judgment.

KNIGHT. I am sorry that it is so late that we must needs depart now.

MERCHANTMAN. CAPPER. HUSBANDMAN. And so be we, in good faith, but we trust, ere you depart the town, to have some communication with you again.

DOCTOR. I will be glad if I tarry in the town.

KNIGHT. And thus we departed for that time. But on the morrow when I knew Master Doctor was gone out of the town, I thought not meet this communication should be lost but remembered at the least in my own private book to the intent, as opportunity should serve, I might bring forth some of his reasons in places where they might either take place, or be answered otherwise than I could; and therefore I have noted the said communication briefly of this sort as you see.

Finis.

APPENDIX A

*Material from
the
First Printed Edition in 1581*

Part 1

The following Epistle Dedicatory appeared after the title in the first published edition of 1581.

To the most virtuous and learned Lady, my most dear and Sovereign Princess Elizabeth, by the Grace of God Queen of England, France, and Ireland; Defendress of the Faith; &c.

Whereas there was never anything heard of in any age past hitherunto, so perfectly wrought and framed, either by art or nature, but that it has at some time, for some forged and surmised matter, sustained the reprehension of some envious persons or other; I do not much marvel, most mighty Princess, that in this your so noble & famous a government, the glory whereof is now long since scattered and spread over the whole face of the earth, there are, notwithstanding, certain evil-disposed people, so blinded with malice and subdued to their own partial conceits that as yet they can neither spare indifferent judgments to conceive, or reverent tongues to report, a known truth, touching the perfection of the same. But for these men, as they are, no doubt, sufficiently refuted by the testimonies of their own consciences, so are they most certainly condemned by the common consent of all such as are wise or indifferent. And although this be of itself so clear and manifest that it cannot be denied, yet could I not forbear, most renowned Sovereign, being as it were enforced by your Majesty's late & singular clemency in pardoning certain my undutiful misdemeanor, but seek to acknowledge your gracious goodness and bounty toward me by exhibiting unto you this small and simple present. Wherein, as I have endeavored in few words to answer certain quarrels and objections, daily and ordinarily occurrent in the talk of sundry men, so do I most humbly crave your Grace's favorable acceptation thereof; protesting also, with all humility, that my meaning is not, in the discourse of these matters here disputed, to define ought which may in any wise sound prejudicial to any public authority, but only to allege such probability as I could, to stop the mouths of certain evil-affected persons which, of their curiosity, require farther satisfaction in these matters than can well stand with good modesty. Wherefore as upon this zeal & good meaning toward your estate, I was earnestly moved to undertake this enterprise and in the handling thereof rather content to show myself unskillful to others than unthankful to you. So, presuming of your ancient accustomed clemency, I was so bold to commit the same to your gracious protection, fully persuading and assuring myself that it would generally obtain the better credit & entertainment among others if your Majesty's name were prefixed as it were a most rich jewel and rare ornament to beautify and commend the same. God preserve Your Majesty with infinite increase of all his blessings bestowed upon you and grant that your days of life here upon the earth may be extended, if it be His good will, even far beyond the ordinary course of nature; that, as you have already sufficiently reigned for your own honor and glory to last with all posterities, so you may continue and remain with us many more years even to the full contentation, if it may so be, of us your loving subjects and to the perfect establishing of this flourishing peace & tranquillity in your commonweal forever.

Your Majesty's
most faithful and
loving subject,
W. S.[1]

[1] See below, *n.* 1 in Appendix B.

Part II

In the first published edition in 1581, the following addition to the *Third Dialogue* replaced the section ** p. 102 to ** page 116.

KNIGHT. If this were the chiefest cause of the dearth, as of very good probability (by you, Master Doctor) heretofore alleged it should seem to be, how comes it to pass (where, as you say, if the cause be removed the effect is also taken away) that the prices of all things fall not back to their old rate whereas now long since our English coin (to the great honor of our noble Princess which now reigns) has been again thoroughly restored to his former purity and perfection?

DOCTOR. Indeed, sir, I must needs confess unto you (although it may seem at the first sight to discredit my former sayings in some part) that notwithstanding that our coin at this present day, yea, and many years past, has recovered his ancient goodness, yet the dearth of all things, which I before affirmed to have proceeded of the decay thereof, to remain and continue still amongst us. Wherefore as your doubt herein, moved very aptly and to the purpose, is well worthy the consideration, so do I account it of such difficulty that perhaps it would not be thought to stand with modesty to undertake without further study presently to dissolve the same.

KNIGHT. Sir, I pray you for this time omit the pleading of modesty. I understand well enough by your former talk that you are not unprovided of sufficient store, without further deliberation, to satisfy us withal, in greater matters if need were than these.

DOCTOR. Well, I am content, because you will have it so, to yield to your importunity. I will utter frankly unto you by opinion herein, but under protestation that, if you like it not, you reject it, imparting likewise with me your own fantasies and judgments in the same. I find therefore two special causes, in my opinion, by means of the which, notwithstanding that restitution made in our coin, the aforesaid dearth of things in respect of the former age remains yet among us. The first is, that whereas, immediately after the baseness of our coin in the time of King Henry the Eight, the prices of all things generally among all sorts of people rose, it must needs happen here withal, as you know, that our gentlemen which lived only upon the revenues of their lands were as near or nearer touched (as is before proved) with the smart hereof than any other, of what order or estate soever. This therefore being taken as most true, the gentlemen, desirous to maintain their former credit in bearing out the port[1] of their predecessors, were driven of necessity as often as whensoever any leases devised for term of years, by themselves or their ancestors, were thoroughly expired and fell into their hands, not to let them out again, for the most part, but as the rents of them were far racked beyond the old. Yea, this racking and hoisting up of rents has continued ever since that time until this present day. Hereupon the husbandman was necessarily enforced, whereas his rent was now greater than before and so continues unto this day, to sell his victuals dearer and to continue the dearth of them; and likewise other artificers withal to maintain the like proportion in their wares. Wherefore as this dearth at the first time, as I said before, sprang of the alteration of the coin as

---

[1] *Port:* income, style and standard of living.

of his first and chiefest cause, so do I attribute the continuance of it, hitherunto and so forward, partly to the racked and stretched rents which have lasted, yea, and increased ever since that time hitherunto, and so are like to continue I know not how long. Now if we would in these days have the old pennyworths generally restored among us again, the restoring of our good coin, which already is past and, before the improved rents, would only of itself have been sufficient to have brought this matter to pass, will not serve in these our days except withal the racked rents be pulled down; which possibly cannot be without the common consent of our landed men throughout the whole realm. Another reason I conceive in this matter to be the great store and plenty of treasure which is walking in these parts of the world, far more in these our days than ever our forefathers have seen in times past. Who does not understand of the infinite sums of gold and silver which are gathered from the Indies and other countries and so yearly transported unto these coasts? As this is otherwise most certain, so does it evidently appear by the common report of all ancient men living in these days. It is their constant report that in times past, and within the memory of man, he has been accounted a rich and wealthy man and well able to keep house among his neighbors which, all things discharged, was clearly worth thirty or forty pounds; but in these our days the man of that estimation is so far (in the common opinion) from a good housekeeper, or man of wealth, that he is reputed the next neighbor to a beggar. Wherefore these two reasons seemed unto me to contain in them sufficient probability for causes of the continuance of this general dearth.

KNIGHT. Yea, but, sir, if the increase of treasure be partly the occasion of this continued dearth, then, by likelihood, in other our neighbors' nations, unto whom yearly is conveyed great store of gold and silver, the prices of victuals and other wares in like sort is raised according to the increase of their treasure?

DOCTOR. It is even so; and therefore, to utter freely mine opinion, as I account it a matter very hard, for the difficulties above rehearsed, to revoke or call back again all our English wares unto their old prices, so do I not take it to be either profitable or convenient for the realm, except we would wish that our commodities should be uttered good cheap to strangers and theirs, on the other side, dear unto us; which could not be without great impoverishing of the Commonweal in a very short time.

APPENDIX B

Relationship of Texts

Part I

The four discovered manuscript texts of the *Discourse* are:
1. The Lambarde MS.
2. The Yelverton MS B.M. Add. MS 48047 ff. 174–227.
3. The Bodleian MS Add. C. 273.
4. The Hatfield MS 269/2.

A collation of the four manuscript texts and the 1581 printed edition reveals very clearly the following relationship of the four texts and the 1581 edition.[1]

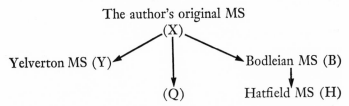

The author's original MS
(X)

Yelverton MS (Y)   Bodleian MS (B)

(Q)   Hatfield MS (H)

This represents an unknown draft from which, it can be shown, "W. S." copied his version for the 1581 edition. This was also the source of the Lambarde MS.

Lambarde MS (L)   Printed 1581 edition
by "W. S." (S)

[1] It should be noted that there were two or three later editions of the 1581 printing, still carrying the 1581 date. These are definitely new printings altering certain words and amending some obvious errors in the first edition. These editions (frequently catalogued as the 1581 edition) are later, one even picking up Anthony à Wood's suggestion of William Stafford's authorship and substituting this for "W. S." on the title page and in the Dedication. Any references given here are to the original 1581 edition as reprinted by F. J. Furnivall in the New Shakspere Soc., Ser. VI, No. 3 (1876).

This diagram emerges from the following observations and conclusions.

The Relationship of (S) to (L) and of (SL) to (YBH)

1. The 1581 printed edition (S) has several obvious *errors*, including simple copyist errors, in common with the Lambarde MS (L) which are not to be found in the Yelverton MS (Y), the Bodleian MS (B), or the Hatfield MS (H). Frequently these common errors make nonsense of the text or obviously less sense than the reading in (YBH).

e.g. (a) p. 61, l. 33. (SL) read "and in a plentiful year no more than enough" which makes nonsense of the point being made. (YBH) all have the clearly correct "and in a plentiful year with more than enough."

e.g. (b) p. 88, l. 9. (SL) read "intend" where (YBH) have the better reading "invent."

e.g. (c) p. 27, l. 35. (SL) read "the conjunct of man's life" not "conduct" as (YBH) do.

2. (S) and (L) have many common *omissions*, sometimes of whole phrases which are found in (YBH).

e.g. (a) p. 48, l. 14. (SL) omit "than the dearth has risen at either of your hands."

e.g. (b) p. 81, l. 6. (SL) both omit "of that which makes best shift."

e.g. (c) p. 23, l. 23. (SL) both omit "in this realm."

3. (S) and (L) share *numerous alternative readings* to (YBH), not necessarily errors but simply a different choice of words. Some of these are important, frequently they are trivial, often it is merely a question of word order which they have in common, or the common use of insignificant pronouns or conjunctions.

e.g. (a) p. 53, l. 4. (SL) read "short time" not "brief time" (YBH).

e.g. (b) p. 59, l. 4. (SL) read "they may be well provoked" not "men may be well provoked" (YBH).

e.g. (c) p. 40, l. 8. (SL) read "have enhanced, any" not "many" (YBH).

4. These links between (S) and (L) point to their use of a common source not used by (YBH). It is clear however that (S) did not copy (L) for the following reasons:

i. (S) has the table of contents and side notes found in (YBH) but not in (L).

ii. (L) has many major *errors* and countless *inaccuracies* which (S) does not have.

e.g. (a) p. 23, l. 11. (L) alone omits "lack of" which is necessary to the sense of the phrase, common to (SYBH), "and all for lack of bodily exercise."

e.g. (b) p. 47, l. 2. (L) alone reads "enhance" where the obviously correct reading is "exhaust" (SYBH).

e.g. (c) p. 45, l. 23. (L) alone puts the sentence beginning "What other things . . ." at the beginning of the Knight's speech; (SYBH) all have it as the last sentence of the Doctor's speech.

e.g. (d) p. 11, l. 23. (L) alone reads "And therefore perchance though they be never so wise" instead of the correct "And therefore princes . . ." (SYBH).

iii. (L) has many *omissions*, of varying importance, where (S) has the words to be found in (YBH).

e.g. (a) p. 32, ll. 8–10. (L) alone omits the passage "On my faith . . . methought."

e.g. (b) p. 13, ll. 8–9. (L) alone omits "to go to the matter . . ." before "that kind of reasoning."

e.g. (c) p. 20, ll. 26–27. (L) alone omits the words "wherein the freemen . . . relieved, how."

iv. (S) has many common readings with (YBH) where (L) has its own, almost invariably less good reading.

e.g. (a) p. 121, ll. 12–20. (SYBH) all attribute this speech to the Merchant; (L) alone attributes it to the Knight.

e.g. (b) p. 25, l. 24. (L) alone reads "unapt for the war" whereas (SYBH) have the obviously better "apt."

e.g. (c) p. 31, l. 24. Instead of the (SYBH) reading "I speak so much of the commendation of learning not only be-

cause I heard my friend here, the capper, set little by learning," (L) alone reads "I speak not much of the common
trade of learning."

Where (S) has these affinities (i, ii, iii, iv) with (YBH)
and not (L), one can properly assume that (S) copied correctly from (Q) which in turn had copied correctly from
(X)–i.e., the source used by (YBH)–but that (L) on the
other hand failed to copy (Q) correctly or deliberately in-
dulged in a freer individual handling of the text.

The relationship of (S) to the (YBH) MSS comes solely
from the accord between (Q) and (X). (S) did not see
either (Y), (B), (H), or (X). This is further confirmed by
an examination of the three MSS (Y), (B), and (H).

THE RELATIONSHIP OF (B) AND (H)

1. (B) and (H) can for all practical purposes be considered
as the same text.

i. They have exactly similar, highly individual, readings
of certain passages very different from the versions in (S),
(L), or (Y).

e.g. (a) p. 116, l. 4. (BH) read "coin new corrected"
instead of "now current" (YL).

e.g. (b) p. 136, l. 23. (BH) read "concerning both of
us" instead of "touching partly the one and partly the
other" (YL).

e.g. (c) p. 7, l. 23. (BH) read "What do strangers bring us
in chief commodities for our treasure" not "What do strangers bring us for our treasure and chief commodities" (SY).

e.g. (d) p. 63, l. 10. (BH) insert "and wrought" between
"made" and "within."

ii. They have several significant common omissions of
words, or whole phrases, not found in (SYL).

e.g. (a) p. 48, ll. 33–34. (BH) omit "that the one has to
pay the other of equal value" (SYL).

e.g. (b) p. 121, ll. 23–24. (BH) omit "in the said towns
. . . wealth" (SYL).

e.g. (c) p. 103, ll. 4–6. (BH) omit "How mean you . . ." down to ". . . another" (YL).

e.g. (d) p. 122, l. 38–p. 123, l. 2. (BH) omit from "hats . . ." down to ". . . girdles" (SYL).

iii. They have common errors and scribal slips not found in (SYL).

e.g. (a) p. 29, l. 10. (BH) betray a common ignorance of Vitruvius, writing "Vegetius."

e.g. (b) p. 38, ll. 19–20. (BH) put the last sentence of the Knight's speech beginning "This is a marvelous dearth" onto the beginning of the next speech of the Doctor where (SYL) have it obviously in the correct place.

e.g. (c) p. 88, l. 1. (BH) read "equity" where the sense is clearly better served by the "quiet" of (SYL).

iv. They have minor emendations in common not found in (SYL).

e.g. (a) p. 21, l. 15. (BH) alone insert "time" in the phrase "than of old [time] was used."

e.g. (b) p. 21, l. 15. (BH) alone has "of the same" for "thereof" (SYL).

e.g. (c) p. 91, l. 5. (BH) alone has "for the breed of men" instead of "nourishment of men" (SYL).

e.g. (d) p. 43, l. 5. (BH) alone has "compelled" for "commanded" (SYL).

2. There is no doubt that (H) derives directly from (B) and not (B) from (H). This emerges from the following points:

i. There are instances where (B) has the same text as (SYL) but (H) alone has an omission.

e.g. (a) p. 30, ll. 23–24. Only (H) omits the words "And these arts be the seven liberal sciences" (BSYL).

e.g. (b) p. 90. Only (H) omits "treasure" in the marginal note "One brings out our treasure" (SYB).
In particular (H) omits almost all passages in Latin whereas (B) has the Latin text common to (SYL).

e.g. (a) p. 91, ll. 7–8.

e.g. (b) p. 92, l. 25.

ii. (H) has a few individual errors not to be found in any other text.

e.g. (a) p. 134, l. 30. (H) alone has "collection" instead of the correct "collation" of (BSYL).

e.g. (b) (H) alone repeats the large section from "wrought here" p. 87, l. 30 down to "subsidies" p. 89, l. 29, a scribal error.

iii. Very occasionally (H) introduces a very minor improvement on (B) where (B) has the reading common to (SYL).

e.g. (a) p. 80, l. 7. (H) alone has "dear after" not "thereafter."

e.g. (b) p. 127, l. 16. (H) alone uses "above" instead of "inferior unto" (BSYL).

e.g. (c) p. 84, l. 29. (H) alone uses "spent" for "swept" (BSYL). There are however *no* examples of (B) having an individual rendering of any passage which is not followed by (H) and on *no* occasion does (H) have a reading in common with (S), (L), and (Y)–i.e., with (X) or (Q)– where (B) does not. It should be noted that the last folio of (B) is now missing. This loss must have taken place after (H) copied the work, for (H) is complete.

3. None of the errors common to (S) and (L) alone–which derive from their mutual use of (Q)–are to be found in (BH); another piece of evidence showing that (B) was using (X) and was not acquainted with (Q).

THE RELATIONSHIP OF (BH) TO (S)

1. (S) was not familiar [2] with (B) or (H). On no occasion does (S) echo any of their individual errors, omissions, emendations or free renderings in several sentences. However as (S) has both the side notes and the table of contents which (Y) and (BH) have, one must assume that (Q) and

---

[2] Contrary to E. Lamond's conjectures on the sources of the printed edition of 1581, *op. cit.*, pp. xxxvi–xxxvii.

(X) both had these and the omission of them in (L) was a deliberate omission by the scribe, another instance of the slipshod and extremely free hand the "Lambarde" scribe took with his text. They were obviously part of the original manuscript and not, as E. Lamond conjectured, an improvement added to the text by (B).

2. Wherever (S) has the same reading as (BH) as opposed to (L), the same reading occurs almost invariably in (Y), emphasizing once again the pattern

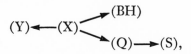

$$(Y)\longleftarrow(X)\begin{array}{c}\nearrow(BH)\\\searrow(Q)\longrightarrow(S),\end{array}$$

where (L) has introduced his own individual reading.

THE YELVERTON MS (Y)

(Y) has a direct relationship with (X) and was not known to (L) or (S) or (BH). (Y) did not know or use (L), (S), or (BH). This emerges from the following points:

i. There is no instance of (Y) following an (L) reading unless this is also to be found in (S)–i.e., in (Q), i.e., in (X). None of the errors, omissions, or individual readings of (L) alone, or (S) alone, or (BH) alone are to be found in (Y).

ii. (Y) has some minor individual errors not to be found anywhere else.

e.g. (a) p. 35, l. 16. (Y) alone misreads "coin" and writes "commons" which makes nonsense of the sentence.

e.g. (b) p. 21, l. 11. (Y) alone has "lands as come to your hands" instead of the correct (SLBH) reading "our hands."

e.g. (c) p. 98, l. 16. (Y) alone has "to take farms to their lands" instead of the obviously correct (SLBH) reading "their hands."

iii. (Y) has several minor individual stylistic improvements and emendations not to be found in (S), (L), or (BH).

e.g. (a) p. 64, l. 18. Only (Y) omits "not" in "there were [not] of these" which is clearly a minor improvement, (SLBH) all have "not." In the same sentence, l. 19, (Y) alone changes "things" to "like."

e.g. (b) p. 39, l. 2. Only (Y) reads "enhance your rents"; (SLBH) read "enhance your lands."

e.g. (c) p. 46, l. 26. Only (Y) has "list"; (SLBH) all read "ask."

It should be noted that these are very minor emendations indeed, not the deliberately free renderings which mark the other texts.

iv. (Y) has a few individual omissions, again minor, which are not to be found in (S), (L), or (BH).

e.g. (a) p. 63, ll. 1–2. (Y) omits "till the price . . . commodities" which (SLBH) all have.

e.g. (b) p. 49, ll. 8–10. (Y) alone omits the phrase "to one man's hand . . . beforetimes." As in the example above, this is clearly a scribal error, the copyist's eye slipped from the first "now," l. 8, down to the second "now," l. 10.

e.g. (c) p. 76, l. 12. (Y) alone omits the phrase "and the ounce with the mark of the ounce," another scribal error where the eye has drifted down from the first "mark of the," l. 11, to the second "mark of the" on l. 12.

v. (Y) is however remarkably free from the numerous and obvious errors of (L) or (S), yet it is closer to the (SL) texts than to the (BH) texts which emerged from the "improving hand" of (B) which again argues a far closer relationship to the original MS (X) than any of the other texts.

Part II

Since this book was sent to the press a fifth manuscript of the *Discourse,* hitherto completely unknown, emerged in the 1967 sale in London of some of the Phillipps collection of manuscripts. This manuscript is now in the possession of the State University of New York at Albany, and I am extremely grateful for the permission, so readily given me by the University, to examine their new acquisition.

The Albany MS is entitled *A Discourse of the Common Welthe of England.* It is not complete; the last thousand words or so are missing, other pages are loose. There is no table of contents, but there are incomplete side notes. An examination of the text leads to the following conclusions:

1. The Albany MS (A) does not derive from, nor is it the source of (Y), (BH), (L), or (S). It has errors, omissions, additions, and alternative readings peculiar to it and not found elsewhere, and it does not repeat any of the distinctive lone readings of (Y), (BH), (L), or (S).

2. (A) has, however, extremely interesting links with the Lambarde MS (L) and the printed edition of 1581 (S), all of which can be explained by the following, slightly amended diagram of the four MSS pattern:

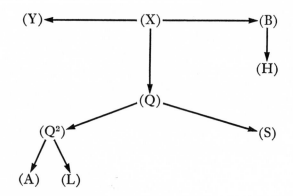

This pattern emerges from:

1. There are many common links of (A), (L), and (S) not found in (YBH). These include:

   i. Common errors of (ALS):

   e.g. (a) p. 88, l. 9. (ALS) have "intend" not the obviously correct (YBH) "invent."

   e.g. (b) p. 27, l. 35. (ALS) have "conjunct" not "conduct" (YBH).

   e.g. (c) p. 40, l. 8. (ALS) have "any" for the obviously more correct "many" (YBH).

   ii. Common omissions of (ALS) not found in (YBH):

   e.g. (a) p. 81, l. 6. (ALS) omit "of that which makes best shift" after "short."

   e.g. (b) p. 48, l. 14. (ALS) omit "than the dearth has risen at either of your hands."

   e.g. (c) p. 35, ll. 3–4. (ALS) omit "at the most, till" before "now of late."

   iii. Common alternative readings of (ALS) to (YBH):

   e.g. (a) p. 29, l. 24. (ALS) read "govern" not "guide" (YBH).

   e.g. (b) p. 53, l. 4. (ALS) read "short" not "brief" (YBH).

   e.g. (c) p. 38, l. 17. (ALS) read "and yet there is scarcity" instead of the far better "it is scarcity" (YBH).

The (ALS) version indeed makes nonsense of the point being made that there is *no* scarcity of anything in this "marvelous dearth that in such plenty comes."

These are only a few examples pointing to an unmistakable definite common source for (A), (L), and (S) —i.e., (Q) —with no acquaintance directly for (A), (L), or (S) with (YBH) —i.e., (X).

Further confirmation of the (Q^2) pattern comes from:

$$(Q^2) \nearrow (A) \searrow (L)$$

2. Examination of (A) throws much light on the way-ward erratic nature of the Lambarde text (L); for not only do (A) and (L) and (S) have several less good renderings or outright errors in common deriving from (Q), but (A) and (L) have even *more* common errors, omissions, and alternative readings not found in (S), who, going back directly to (Q), was spared these (Q^2) errors, etc.

   i. Common errors of (AL) not found in (SYBH):

   e.g. (a) p. 47, l. 2. Only (AL) read "enhance" instead of the clearly correct "exhaust" (SYBH).

   e.g. (b) p. 78, l. 22. Only (AL) read "ships" instead of "heaps" (SYBH).

   e.g. (c) p. 31, l. 24. Only (AL) read "common trade" of learning, not the clearly correct "commendation" (SYBH).

   ii. Common omissions of (AL) not found in (SYBH):

   e.g. (a) p. 32, ll. 8–10. Only (AL) omit the sentence at the beginning of the Knight's speech "On my faith, I am glad it was my chance to have you in my company at this time. For of a wise man a man may always learn. But methought . . ." (SYBH). Both (A) and (L) begin the speech "You said ere while . . . ."

   e.g. (b) p. 13, ll. 8–9. Only (AL) omit the phrase "to go to the matter upon boldness of your good acceptance" after "Therefore now . . . ."

   e.g. (c) p. 23, l. 11. Only (AL) omit the vital words

"lack of" in the phrase "all for lack of bodily exercise," thus making nonsense of the whole sentence.

    iii. Common alternative readings of (AL) to (SYBH):

    e.g. (a) p. 51, l. 2. Only (AL) add "the more is the pity" at the end of the sentence ". . . as we see they do now too fast."

    e.g. (b) p. 29. l. 3. Only (AL) add "and housing of the same" after "your corn and grass" and before "housing of your cattle."

    e.g. (c) Countless examples of one word differences:

    (1) p. 13, l. 3. (AL) "spoken," (SYBH) "touched."

    (2) p. 13, ll. 3-4. (AL) "disputation," (SYBH) "disceptation."

    (3) p. 22, l. 6. (AL) "ago," (SYBH) "past."

    (4) p. 28, l. 20. (AL) "things," (SYBH) "sciences."

    (5) p. 76, l. 16. (AL) "advertised," (SYBH) "assured."

These common (AL) links point to a common source (Q^2) where $(A)=(L)$, i.e., (Q^2) but (S) going through $(Q)=$ (YBH) (X). However (A) was a better and more accurate transcriber than (L), and though (A) has these errors in common with (L) where they are both copying (Q^2), (A) has far fewer extra errors and careless free renderings *of its own* than does (L). The Lambarde MS (L) remains, with (Q) errors and (Q^2) errors and its own carelessness, the MS most full of errors, omissions, and readings straying away from the original text.

    This pattern of $(AL)=(Q^2)$ and $(ALS)=(Q)$ is completely confirmed it should be noted by two major points:

    1. At no point in the text does $(A)=(S)$ where $(L)=$ (YBH).

    2. At no point in the text does $(S)=(L)$ where $(A)=$ (YBH). The common lone (AS) readings only occur where (L) has gone off alone and $(A)=(Q^2)=(Q)=(S)$. The common lone (SL) readings only occur where (A) has gone off alone and $(L)=(Q^2)=(Q)=(S)$. Further confirmation of the pattern

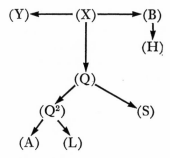

comes from a study of the marginal notes of the MSS and of (S). Although (A) and (L) both omit the table of contents—as presumably did (Q²)—which (S) derived from (Q), (A) unlike (L) does not omit the side notes which (Q²) must have copied from (Q). Although (A)'s side notes have frequent omissions and are occasionally casual laconic renderings of the full side notes found in (S) and (YBH), they give further confirmation of the over-all pattern of the MSS; for in those instances where (S) has a different side-note reading from (BH), then (AYS) are found to agree. Where (Y) and (BH) have the same marginal-note reading but (S) is different, we now find that in these instances (S) invariably equals (A), confirming their common source in (Q). One example of this should suffice:

e.g. p. 90. (A) and (S) both read "Three sorts of Artificers," not (YBH)'s "Three sorts of mysteries."

The Albany MS has one further point of interest. On the first page there is a note in a late sixteenth-century or early seventeenth-century hand "I thinke it not fit that this Treatize be printed, except it be authorised by some of the Lordes of the Consayle. Tho: London." The *Discourse* was written in 1549 and first published in 1581. The "Tho. London" must refer to a Bishop of London acting as one of the censors to whom all publications were submitted. There is no Bishop of London between 1549 and 1581 bearing the Christian name "Thomas." The only possible explanation seems to be the rather odd one that when Thomas Ravis was Bishop of London, in 1607–1609, some owner of the (A) manuscript submitted it to him and neither he, nor the Bishop, were aware that it had already been published in 1581.